Love Your food"!

Carol L. Horgan CEC

THE
LIGHTHOUSE BREAKFAST
COOKBOOK

Published by WestWinds Press®

An imprint of Graphic Arts Center Publishing Company

P.O. Box 10306, Portland, Oregon 97296-0306

503-226-2402 www.gacpc.com

Library of Congress Cataloging-in-Publication Data:

Bursey, Michelle.

The lighthouse breakfast cookbook : recipes from Heceta Head Lighthouse Bed and Breakfast / Michelle Bursey and Carol Korgan ; photography by Tim Mantoani.

p. cm.

Includes index.

ISBN 978-0-88240-743-2 (softbound)

1. Breakfasts. 2. Heceta Head Lighthouse Bed and Breakfast. I. Korgan, Carol. II. Title.

TX733.B97 2009

641.5'2—dc22

2008047852

President: Charles M. Hopkins

Associate Publisher: Douglas A. Pfeiffer

Editorial Staff: Timothy W. Frew, Jean Andrews, Kathy Howard, Jean Bond-Slaughter

Production Coordinator: Heather Doornink

Editor: Sue Mann

Designer: Jamison Design/J. Spittler

Printed in the United States of America

Steven Bursey wishes to acknowledge the following sources for the section about the history of Heceta Head:

Finucane, Stephanie. "Heceta House: A History and Architectural Survey." In *Studies in Cultural Resource Management* No. 3, Waldport Ranger District, Waldport, Oregon. Forest Service—USDA Pacific Northwest Region Siuslaw National Forest. Printed jointly by Lane Community College and the USFS for the Heceta House Development Fund, 1985.

"Heceta Head: A Light Station Odyssey Part I." *The Keeper's Log*, Spring 1992, Vol. VIII No. 3, published by the U.S. Lighthouse Service.

"Heceta Head: A Light Station Odyssey Part II." *The Keeper's Log*, Summer 1992, Vol. VIII No. 4, published by the U.S. Lighthouse Service.

McCracken, Theresa. "Heceta Head Light Station: A History of Its People and Buildings." This article was never published. The researched was commissioned by the USFS in 1997.

Personal conversations and interview as recorded by the author Steven Bursey in his capacity as docent and interpretive director over the past ten years.

THE LIGHTHOUSE BREAKFAST COOKBOOK

Recipes from
HECETA HEAD LIGHTHOUSE
BED & BREAKFAST

MICHELLE BURSEY AND CAROL KORGAN CEC
PHOTOGRAPHY BY TIM MANTOANI

WESTWINDS PRESS®

To Mother and Grandmother Marie Codr,
our inspiration and guardian.
We miss you.

CONTENTS

ACKNOWLEDGMENTS

MICHELLE

How do you begin to thank everyone for a project that took eight years? I have to start with our guests—their constant e-mails, demands from the breakfast table, and cheers of glee when we finally started getting serious—without whom this cookbook never would have happened.

Then the amazing support system of friends and family who have encouraged me when I felt it was much bigger than anything I could put a lasso around and tie down. I don't think I'll get the best timing at the rodeo, but I am throwing my hat to a cheering crowd and all I have to say is, Yee haw, we did it!

Tim, thank you for working with us on this project and being so generous with your time. Your photographs make me blush! Lisa; Kim; Kim's mom, Carol; and Lora: special thanks for reading and testing our first attempts at writing recipes.

Having never done something like this, Mom and I didn't know what we were getting into, and what started as a once-a-week meeting ended up becoming a month-and-a-half stay at my parents' house. I allowed myself visitation rights to my husband and son. During that time my very patient husband, Steven, and super inn manager, Kim, held down the fort and really did an exemplary job; for this I am deeply thankful. And I am also thankful to be back building plans with Steven, cooking with Kim, and working with the best crew ever. I love my job!

And finally to my parents: Dad, you were the muse for every recipe. Thank you for creating such a wonderful breakfast. Thank you for allowing Mom and me to honor your idea and put this work together. You've always had the best ideas, and I feel privileged to take what you started and see it bloom and grow. Thank you for raising me in a way that would give me the necessary tools.

Mom, I have learned so much from you. To date this book has been the biggest challenge and biggest achievement for me; had it not been for you, I would still be sitting and writing and not having much fun at all. Thank you for the silly conversations, the heated culinary debates, and the hours of testing and retesting and helping resist the temptation of just bagging it and playing cards. I've always known it, but this time together has really sealed the deal. You are my best friend.

MICHELLE BURSEY

CAROL

I want to thank my friends and family, who always gave me encouragement, and my sons, Dan and Todd, both fabulous chefs on whom I could always count.

I want to thank my dear, wonderful husband, Mike, for always believing in me, encouraging me, and giving his full support. He convinced me that we could open and run a restaurant. He was the driving force, writing menus twice a day, purchasing the food, and entering food exhibitions, chocolate con-

tests, and food competitions—and he knew that if we studied and worked hard we could become certified executive chefs. He put together our resumes and applied to open the B&B at Heceta Head. It was his idea to serve the seven-course breakfast. He taught me a lot, and we learned a lot together about food. I want to thank him for teaching me "First you eat with your eyes." I love you.

Last and most important, Michelle heard all her life, "There's going to be a cookbook."

She made this happen. I wouldn't trade the time we had together for anything in the world: testing, resizing, and reconstructing recipes. She has a magical sense about food, from her palate to her ability to make food look beautiful. Her determination, research, and many many hours of getting it all down on paper have made a dream come true.

Thank you, Michelle and Steven, for continuing with Heceta Head B&B, bringing so much joy and comfort to the many people who visit that beautiful historic landmark.

CAROL LEE KORGAN, CEC

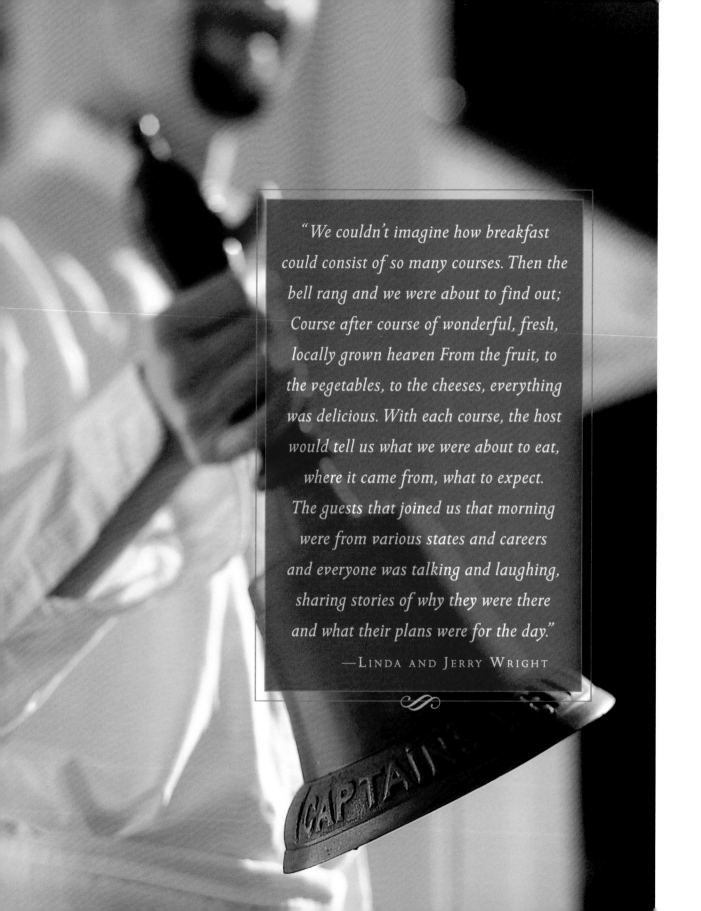

"We couldn't imagine how breakfast could consist of so many courses. Then the bell rang and we were about to find out; Course after course of wonderful, fresh, locally grown heaven From the fruit, to the vegetables, to the cheeses, everything was delicious. With each course, the host would tell us what we were about to eat, where it came from, what to expect. The guests that joined us that morning were from various states and careers and everyone was talking and laughing, sharing stories of why they were there and what their plans were for the day."

—LINDA AND JERRY WRIGHT

INTRODUCTION

I have had the pleasure and privilege of preparing the seven-course breakfast at Heceta Head for 10 years. Preparing this breakfast is the highlight of my day and the best part of my job. It is my creative outlet. It is a way to spread joy and foster an environment that allows people to enjoy the goodness of food, conversation, and camaraderie. I feel privileged to cater to a crowd that has chosen Heceta Head to celebrate big moments in their lives: anniversaries, weddings, or milestone birthdays. It is really satisfying to know that people have chosen to come to Heceta Head for a much needed break from life's challenges and that they will find not only a magical lighthouse experience but also a meal unlike any they have ever had.

Food for me is remembering. It starts with remembering where the food came from and how it was cultivated. It ends with remembering all life's wonderful times and connecting them to meals that seal those memories. And in between there is a colorful spectrum of comforts and creative inspirations that fill my culinary palette. This book is an extension of those feelings. It is the culmination of years working with my parents at their restaurant in Portland; traveling in the States, Southeast Asia, Europe and Mexico; reading and learning from accomplished chefs; and decades of wonderful family meals and celebrations.

Writing the book was a huge challenge for my mother and me because we come from the school of "add a little of this and a little of that" until the dish is just right. Quantifying into exact proportions was not an easy task for us, but the results were rewarding. We hope you not only enjoy making these recipes but you also try to keep the "little of this and a little of that" philosophy. We like to work with foods available seasonally, use local ingredients, and share with our friends the specialties of the coast, Oregon, and the Northwest. Every place on the planet has unique ingredients to celebrate. Seek them out wherever you may be and add them to your recipes. Celebrate your local artisan food producers and small farmers; their products will make your guests feel pampered and special as well as make meals to remember.

We hope you enjoy making the dishes included at our seven-course breakfast and reading the stories that make every dish special. In the following pages you will find a little history about my parents and how Steven and I came to Heceta Head. Also, we are proud to share an intriguing history of Heceta Head written by Steven Bursey. Finally in the back of the book you will find a few sections that may be of special use. We have a section on "The Basics," recipes that are common to our kitchen or often repeated in the book. In particular we encourage you to read "kitchen insights" before making any of our recipes. Following "The Basics" we provide a "glossary" of ingredients we use which may not be familiar and a resource guide that will lead you in the direction to find the unique ingredients we highlight.

Enjoy! We hope this book inspires you to create meals that are the highlight of your day.

MICHELLE BURSEY

In a one-room schoolhouse in the 1950s at the edge of a sweeping Nebraska prairie, an idea was born, the brainchild of the only student in her sixth-grade class, a girl who'd grown up catching and dressing chickens on her parents' 180-acre farm. By her mother's side she prepared harvesttime feasts—meals her family talked about for weeks afterward as their mouths watered.

Eleven-year-old Carol Lee was dismayed that her classmates were bringing cold, brown-bagged lunches to school, deprived of something warm and hearty when outside it was not uncommon for the temperature to be 10 below zero in the wintertime. Little did she know it, but Carol Lee was about to land her first job.

"I approached the teacher and said it'd be a really good idea if we got all the kids to bring cans of soup to school," Carol Lee remembers.

And they did. Careful to ensure that there were no ill-advised combinations, Carol Lee and a friend trudged into the kitchen in the school's basement, cracked open the cans, poured the contents into a pot, and started a hot new tradition.

This is the part where you find out how it all began; where you learn not only how a farm girl from Nebraska discovered her love of food but how a boy from Oklahoma discovered the very same thing—and how the two of them found each other and how their fondness for food and entertaining grew together with their friends, their children, and eventually their whole community.

As many girls her age did, Carol Lee learned how to cook and sew as a child, but she learned from a mother who had particular flair in the kitchen. Carol Lee's mother Marie was so preoccupied with food that her journal consisted of recipes and, when she was traveling, the contents of each meal they enjoyed. While other mothers were eager to try the latest convenience foods of the 1950s, Marie was particularly interested in keeping with Czech tradition and preserving family heritage. A 4H leader, Marie advocated knowing where foods come from and learning the best ways to cultivate them. "Fresh eggs and cream, homemade sausages and strudels were a part of daily life," and a long-standing tradition not to be compromised. Carol Lee was encouraged to foster those ideas, and although it has been years since she moved from the farm, she has kept those principles sacred.

During her high school years Carol Lee furthered her food knowledge when she took a job at a "very German" restaurant. It may have been a mom-and-pop operation, but it was not the type of place with staff who could proclaim "that's not my job." Carol Lee worked hard to learn everything they would teach her, from the front to the back of the house. The following summer she also worked at Johnson's, a meatpacking plant and community frozen foods locker. There she learned more than just how to butcher farm animals. Johnson's also happened to have a soda fountain and diner in front, a hot spot for the teens. When she wasn't busy helping dress and package beef, she could be found brining broasted chicken or serving up a cherry Coke. Ironically, with her mind set on cosmetology school Carol Lee had no idea those eclectic jobs would one day help her to become the first woman certified executive chef in Oregon.

Carol's mother, Marie.

Mike Korgan grew up on a dairy farm, "at the underfoot of my grandmother," from whom he learned to make German-style noodles shaped "like the state of Tennessee." While his pals were ogling cars, Mike concentrated on "girls and food, in that order. And there was a time, like all little boys, when I didn't like girls." He helped his grandmother in the kitchen and the garden before broadening his horizons at his first kitchen job: a Rexall soda fountain in Oklahoma City.

Hired to wash dishes, Mike was soon learning how to make simple syrup—"the guy was too cheap to buy the premade ones. Now that I look back on it, the product we made was better. He started selling syrups to other fountains and before I knew it I was making 20 to 30 gallons a day." One day the cook didn't show up. The owner pointed at Mike and said, "You."

"For the rest of that summer, I was a short-order cook," Mike said.

He took to it right away. Customers told him, after devouring his Salisbury steak, that he should be a chef. Mike had a few secrets: one was lots of garlic and salt, "that one ingredient that makes food taste good" (and he won't tell us which one!), and two, he wanted to be a radio announcer.

In 1960 Mike and Carol met at an ice-skating rink at the Lincoln, Nebraska, Memorial Coliseum. Some youngsters were getting together for hot chocolate. "When "Carol walked in the room," Mike said. "I decided right then and there that I was going to marry her." Not many months later, he sealed the proclamation with a kiss when they were wed in Council Bluffs, Iowa.

Back in Lincoln Mike was working as program director for the only rock 'n' roll radio station in Lincoln when he got a call from a conglomerate that owned as many radio stations as the federal government allowed—seven. Mike went to Omaha for an interview. "I'm not going to Omaha," was Carol's adamant response.

Instead, they moved to Portland, Oregon, where Mike enjoyed celebrity status on KISN radio as Ken Chase, "the luncheon munchin' kid." Mike worked the noon to 3:00 P.M. slot, and he sponsored a daily contest: he'd list ingredients one by one and invite listeners to call in and guess what he was "making."

With rock 'n' roll all the rage and no regular haunt in Portland for kids to hang out, the Korgans thought it would be fun to open an underage teenage nightclub. The Chase became the hot spot in town. Mike and Carol dished up hamburgers and hot dogs to hungry teenagers, served virgin rum and cokes at their mock bar, and brought the latest local sounds to a packed audience. Mike had an eye not only for entertaining and ambience, but also for talent. The crowds went wild when the bands played a certain song, so Mike took his house band at the time, The Kingsmen, into the recording studio and produced the all-time party song, "Louie Louie," which to this day is considered one of the greatest hits in rock 'n' roll history.

In time the Korgans grew out of the teenage scene and moved into Eastmoreland, a well-established community. They continued entertaining, though, with huge dinner parties and progressive dining parish fund-raisers. More than two hundred people would visit their southeast Portland home in an evening and rave about the goodies Carol prepared. Comments always came back to, "You should open a restaurant." Finally giving in to the plea they decided to go for it, but much to Carol's dismay Mike came home one day with keys to a decrepit little turn-of-the-century bungalow in Sellwood. "It looked as though it hadn't been painted since it was built, and the porch was not only slanted but caving in. I agreed to do it only if I didn't have to do the books or make strudel," remembered Carol. She wound up doing both, but at least the strudel garnered rave reviews.

The summer of 1976 Mike and Carol and their two boys—Dan, 15 and Todd, 14—transformed a sad, overgrown dump into Korgan's Restaurant and Strudel House, a sparkling painted lady. It was a huge hit. Eager customers lined up on the first day. The popularity of the Korgans' Reuben sandwich meant a semi backed up to the eatery each month and unloaded two thousand pounds of corned beef. Before long, the restaurant was a Portland institution.

The entire family worked together to keep the Strudel House hopping for its 18 years. The boys kept the diners happy and dishes clean during their teen years and eventually managed the house and kitchen. Michelle, at the young age of four, learned to peel garlic and separate eggs. Every year meant a new job and more responsibility for her. As she learned and matured so did the restaurant.

Carol and Mike never stopped cultivating their knowledge of food. What started as a really good deli eventually grew to be a stage for the finest regional foods and spirits. The Korgans sought out the best of Oregon, from wild mushrooms to mussels to the newest Oregon Pinot. Whatever they could highlight they would. If they couldn't find something, they often made it themselves—as was the case with coffee. Long before the coffee boom they roasted their own beans and started a micro-roasting company that catered to their restaurant and a select few other fine dining establishments in the Portland area.

In 1993 the Korgans reached a pivotal point in their lives. "We're not wealthy but we're not worried about where our next meal is coming from either," Mike said. "We've got a lot of living to do yet."

They had sold the restaurant and were ready to sell the coffee roasting company. They decided to travel and maybe work as docents or volunteer in places around the country. Then one night they turned on the evening news and watched a broadcast that would change their lives.

The U.S. Forest Service wanted a couple to move to the Oregon Coast and as volunteers help open a bed and breakfast in the keeper's quarters of Heceta Head Lighthouse, where only a ghost resided at the time. The Korgans had never been to Heceta Head and didn't mention much of the story to each other—until the next day.

"I got up, looked at Carol, Carol looked at me and she said, 'I can't get that lighthouse off my mind.' I said, 'You know what? I can't either.'"

The deadline for applications was the following day. Mike quickly crafted a resume and the next day they drove to Waldport, Oregon, where Mike slipped the application under the door. Though thousands sent applications, the Forest Service stopped accepting them after receiving 500. The service conducted extensive interviews and, after rounds of eliminating candidates, the Korgans were chosen.

The Korgans had never stayed in a B&B, but that allowed them to use a fresh approach. They poured hundreds of hours into fixing up the keeper's quarters, opened the B&B on the second floor, and opened the interpretive center on the first floor. Just like with their restaurant, they gained instant

success in many ways. Far from the cares of the modern world, guests are able to stay in the keeper's quarters and relive the life of a lighthouse keeper. In the morning guests are treated to the B&B's opulent seven-course breakfast. Free public tours are given in the summer, which allows many who have always wondered about the keeper's quarters to enter and enjoy its rich history. And money generated from the B&B goes back into the quarters, helping to protect and restore the lightstation.

In the spring of 1998, Mike and Carol's daughter, Michelle, graduated from college, sold her coffee shop, and left her sweetheart, Steven, in Walla Walla, Washington. She went to Heceta Head for the summer to help her parents, give historic tours, and cater weddings. Her ultimate goal was to figure out what was next. She still hasn't left. Instead, she convinced Steven to sell his business, move to Heceta Head, and help run the B&B while her parents took a much-deserved break.

Michelle and Steven agreed to run the B&B for a year and then took six months to travel. They figured that after their return they would live in Seattle—Michelle as a chef and Steven as a waiter—save money, and travel again. But Mike and Carol had a different idea. "Why don't you write up a job description and compensation package and we'll see what we think about it," Steven recalled they had said. "We wrote it out and they said, 'That sounds great. You guys run the business and we'll work for you.'" The Korgans had wanted to retire. Not ones to turn away a once-in-a-lifetime opportunity, Steven and Michelle agreed to take over the business.

In the 10 years since Michelle and Steven have run the B&B, much has changed —especially improving the keeper's house and grounds—but one thing remains the same: the seven-course breakfast. Of particular import was the way the courses were paced, allowing guests to cleanse their palates regularly and enjoy each item thoroughly. Another key element is fresh ingredients, beginning with Steven's raised bed garden, visible from the dining room windows and expanding to include areas nearby. The ingredients are carefully chosen and blended to ensure the most flavorful combinations possible. The eggs come from a farm in nearby Walton; the fruit is handpicked for them at various stands and markets; the cheeses are artisan from local farms.

The breakfast also encourages a social scene and parlor talk experience many people do not have time to engage in these days. "Sitting down for an hour and a half to have a meal and enjoy the company of others is unusual today in the States. It's even torture for a few type As, but to us it is just as beautiful as the ocean and the lighthouse," Michelle reflects. Breakfast commences with a captain's bell calling the guests to gather round a large table that seats up to 14. The rituals begin with guests introducing themselves and telling why they are visiting the lighthouse or something about themselves. Freshly roasted coffee from Schöndecken, the roaster the Korgans started, or a large selection of Oregon Stash teas is served. As the courses are consumed, the conversation starts to percolate and usually halfway into the meal the talk reaches a crescendo and the table is brimming with energy. People exchange ideas; talk of travel, family, and even politics are often discussed in an amicable way. "By the time I go out and say good morning to everyone, there is a certain connection at the table; it seems more like a group than a table of individuals or couples." Michelle regularly witnesses the exchange of maps, home addresses, and e-mail addresses.

There are many plans for the lightstation, both restoration and interpretive. One thing that will not change, however, is the seven-course breakfast.

WRITTEN BY MICHELLE BURSEY AND WINSTON ROSS

FROM THE GUESTS

Tom and Carol Mihok:

"We anticipated cold cereal, cold muffins, and a cold drink to wash it all down," wrote guests Tom and Carol Mihok, who stayed during an electrical outage. "Boy were we surprised. . . .We sat down with the other guests (total of eight) and had the most wonderful, delightful breakfast that my wife and I can ever remember. Everything we had was cooked on the gas range. And except for the 'smoothies' that could not be made, the eggs, bacon, sausage, crepes, and other delights were absolutely scrumptious."

Linda Novakovich:

"The wonderful combination of delicacies in the various courses complemented one another perfectly. The explanations of what each type of dish did for the palate was something I had never experienced before or since. Even more fascinating was the fact that every ingredient is freshly grown in Oregon."

HISTORY OF HECETA HEAD

March 30, 1894, marks the day Heceta Head's five-wick lamp was first ignited—the brightest light on the Oregon Coast. However, her story begins some 60 years earlier when an increasing number of settlers arrived in the 1830s and 1840s, searching for a new life in the Oregon Territory. Some came in search of fertile soil in the land of "milk and honey"; others came to trap furs to export overseas. Missionaries pressed on to the Oregon Territories to build churches and convert the Native Americans. Soon towns and ports were established along the rugged coast, particularly where large rivers flowed into the ocean. Sailing ships ferried passengers and supplies to and from Oregon in increasing numbers. The federal government was keenly aware of the need to establish lighthouses along the Pacific Coast and in 1849 sent a survey team. Sixteen lighthouses were recommended and quickly built. However, the middle of the Oregon Coast was overlooked. As commerce increased along the Siuslaw River, where the town of Florence is now located, more and more mariners had to navigate along that dark stretch of coast between the Siuslaw River and Yaquina Bay. In 1890 the need to ensure safe travel in that area prompted the Lighthouse Board to begin building one final beacon.

Heceta Head was chosen as the site for construction, placing it between Yaquina Head Lighthouse in Newport to the north and the Umpqua River Lighthouse near Reedsport to the south. It was an ideal location for a lighthouse because the light could be seen unobstructed by ships at sea. Congress earmarked $80,000 for the purchase of land, building materials, and labor. In 1891 a presidential order signed by Benjamin Harrison finalized the purchase of land, water rights, and road access to Heceta Head from local homesteaders. Before construction could begin, however, a road had to be carved through the wilderness to connect Heceta Head to the Florence docks 13 miles away. A dirt wagon road that followed an old Native American trail was built along the cliffs. Under the best conditions, it would take a full day to get a wagon load from Florence to the lighthouse worksite. After a rain the wagon driver had to wait a few days for the road to dry out enough to be passable. Brick from San Francisco, stone from the Clackamas River, nails, and dynamite were all hauled in by wagon.

The builders developed a quicker, more reliable way to move building supplies into the area. Anything that could float was loaded onto the tugboat Lillian at the docks in Florence and steamed up the coast to the mouth of Cape Cove Creek below the headlands. On a calm day and with the tide coming in, the floatables were thrown overboard to wash ashore. Waiting laborers picked up the materials. The lumber for construction was logged from old-growth trees up the Siuslaw River, milled in Mapleton, and bundled and sent to the construction site by that method. The Fresnel lens was carefully packed in crates, shipped to Heceta House on a U.S. lighthouse ship or "lighthouse tender," and rowed ashore on a surfboat.

The United States Lighthouse Service hired 56 men to construct the lighthouse. A foreman and bookkeeper kept track of carpenters, masons, laborers, and teamsters. Most of the men bunked in tents, but it was rumored that the foreman built a tree house for himself and spent the evenings swaying alone in the trees. Construction plans from the Umpqua River Lighthouse were used for the tower and the keeper's quarters, possibly in an attempt to save money and expedite construction.

By August 1893 most of the construction was complete. Two beautiful Queen Anne–style keeper's quarters stood overlooking the Pacific Ocean. One was a single dwelling for the head lighthouse keeper and family; the other was a duplex for the first assistant and second assistant lighthouse keepers and their families. Farm animals were housed in a two-story barn near the quarters. At the end of the headland a 56-foot-high lighthouse tower and two oil houses were constructed. A gleaming two-inch thick, hand ground, first order Fresnel lens, built by the Chance Brothers of Birmingham, England, was carefully installed at the top of the tower.

The Fresnel lens was designed by Augustine Fresnel, a Frenchman whose designs revolutionized optics and were applied to lighthouse's optics with great success. The lens rotated on brass chariot wheels, the power supplied by a series of clockwork mechanisms similar to a grandfather clock. As a weight descended the tower, gears slowly rotated the lens. Each lighthouse was given a different signature to allow ship captains to positively identify where they were along the coast. The signature was defined by the color of the lens, the number of light flashes, and the interval between flashes. Heceta Head's signature became one white flash every 10 seconds.

Construction was finished when the oil lamp, shipped from Staten Island, New York, was placed inside the lens. The lamp consisted of five concentric wicks that originally burned refined kerosene. It was very important for the light to be in the exact center of the lens, so a trained installer, also from Staten Island, had to travel to Heceta Head to do the job. This caused a delay in the work, but on March 30, 1894, eight beams of light shone 20 miles out to sea.

Life at Heceta Head at the turn of the century was similar to life on a homestead. The light keepers lived in isolation because of the arduous route to and from Florence. Not many people made the journey to the lighthouse unless they had very good reasons. Although some food was hauled from town and brought in by the lighthouse tender, the majority of food the families either grew or harvested. Large vegetable gardens were planted every year just above the beach and down from the keeper's quarters. Pictures of the gardens show a variety of vegetables, including corn, lettuce, beets, string beans, green onions, and peas. The garden was located close to Cape Creek to provide year- round water, which was a particular concern during the dry summer months. Like many other homesteaders, Annie Hansen, wife of head lighthouse keeper (1904–1920) Olaf Hansen, was an excellent gardener and canned all the vegetables and fruit she could. On the headlands above the lightstation, large flocks of sheep roamed and grazed within a large fenced pasture. Chickens, milk cows, and horses were tended and housed in the barn.

Hunting and fishing were very productive at the turn of the century. The light keepers and local homesteaders hunted throughout the year whether or not it was hunting season. One of the biggest challenges was to evade the local game warden, who made unannounced visits to ensure compliance. His visits were often during dinner when he could check what was on the table. Smelt and salmon runs also provided bountiful tasty feasts.

A small, single-room school was built shortly after construction of the lightstation. During school hours the children would check on Cape Creek, and when the salmon ran they would jump up, grab fishing spears, and head for the creek. It's not recorded what the teachers thought of the practice, but they certainly must have known that any help putting food on the table was necessary.

The women and children took care of most of the domestic work to free the men to work on maintaining the lightstation. The United States Lighthouse Service published a manual detailing the exact standards of care that were expected for every task performed. During the day the light keepers were expected to maintain the station in good working order and be able to pass the white glove test. All buildings were to be free of rust, dust, and debris and properly painted. Equipment was to be polished to a high shine and work flawlessly. A light keeper, asked to describe his job, summed it up by saying, "Chip and paint, chip and paint, chip and paint."

At night the light keepers took turns staffing the tower. An hour before dusk the weights of the clockwork mechanisms were cranked up the tower, the curtain surrounding the lens was opened, the lamp was lit, and the vents were adjusted in accordance to the wind. Throughout the night the light keepers kept an eye on the lamp and the weights, filling the reservoir with oil and winding the weight every four hours. While on shift the men relaxed in the workroom, a small room adjacent to the tower, often reading books next to a small fireplace. The lighthouse service provided a traveling library filled mostly with fiction. Several hundred traveling libraries circulated from lightstation to lightstation.

In exchange for constant and unending work, light keepers were compensated with their lodging, eight cords of wood a year, some food, and a paycheck that varied depending on rank. Head lighthouse keepers were paid $800 a year, First Assistants $600, and Second Assistants $550. At the turn of the century this was considered good pay. The lighthouse service was run much like the military. Men were assigned rank and could be moved from post to post by decision of the service.

A lighthouse inspector stopped by at least once or twice a year to ensure that each station was running smoothly and up to standards; he attempted to make unannounced inspections to determine exactly how things were being run. However, as the inspector traveled up or down the coast, light keepers sent word ahead that he was on his way. Everything was inspected, from the lens in the tower to the cupboards, mantels, and window sills in the keeper's quarters. Keeping the lightstation to the white glove standard at all times was exceedingly difficult. Light inside the homes was from kerosene lamps, which had to be polished daily. Along with the gardening and cooking, women polished, dusted, mopped, cared for the children, and tried to help them keep their things in order. Through it all they hoped the inspector wouldn't catch them unawares. If he found anything out of order, he could reprimand or remove a keeper from his post. A woman was once "cited" for sorting her dirty laundry on the floor.

Despite the threat of such stringent inspections, many light keepers thrived at Heceta Head, which created a comfortable and sustainable environment for all three families.

One such keeper was Cap Herman, a career keeper who arrived at Heceta Head in 1925 and stayed until 1950 as the head light keeper. Cap and his wife, affectionately referred to as Ma, arrived at a time in which not much had changed in the area since 1894. The first big change was the construction during World War I of the Oregon Coast Highway, now Highway 101. It started as a military project to connect the Oregon Coast and protect against a possible foreign invasion. However, it turned into a local project to ease travel and to promote interstate commerce. The motto chosen for the project was "Lift Oregon Out of the Mud", an apt slogan for the rainy coastline. The last part of the Oregon Coast to be paved was the section between Florence and Yachats, a particularly difficult stretch because of the exposed cliffs and numerous streams.

Famed architect Conde McCullough designed the bridge spanning Cape Creek after a Roman aqueduct in France. More than 90 men worked on building the bridge and boring a tunnel through a rocky outcropping. The men lived by the cape in tents and hastily built shacks. Several supervisors moved in with a local homesteader who opened his house to earn a little extra money. The construction project took a little over a year to finish and ended up costing far more than was anticipated. At the time of completion, the tunnel and bridge comprised the most expensive mile on the entire 101 route.

The completion of the Oregon Coast Highway in 1932 drastically changed life at Heceta Head. The days of isolation were over. Day trippers traveled up and down the coast and stopped to tour the lighthouse. The lighthouse service asked Cap to give tours as long as they didn't interfere with his many other official duties. This development pleased Cap very much because he loved to talk and now had an endless supply of listeners. The highway made life a lot easier for the residents at Heceta Head, also. Instead of producing their food, the keepers drove into town for supplies. The school closed and the local children received their education in Florence.

The second big change to the lighthouse came in 1934 with the introduction of electricity. A small garage-shed with several bays was constructed not far from the house. One bay housed a diesel generator that provided power for the lighthouse and the keeper's quarters. In the quarters chandeliers were hung in the dining rooms, parlors, and bedrooms. In the Second Assistant's quarters all the lamps came with four bulbs. As the assistant moved up in rank, another bulb was added, so the lamps in the First Assistant quarters all had five bulbs and the head keeper was blessed with six bulbs. (The living quarters were arranged so that as an assistant moved up in rank he moved closer to the lighthouse as well. It may seem insignificant, but surely it was appreciated when he had to walk to the lighthouse in the middle

of the night during driving rain.) Inside the lighthouse the five-wick lamp was removed and in its place a 500-watt tungsten bulb was installed. The bulb, in combination with the Fresnel lens, produced one million candlepower, a significant improvement from the eighty thousand candlepower the five-wick lamp had previously produced.

Because the introduction of electricity reduced the lighthouse workload so two men could handle everything, the U.S. Coast Guard (which was combined with the lighthouse service in 1939) moved both families into the duplex and the head keeper's house was put up for sale. Whoever bought the

house was required to remove it from the property. The winning bid of $10 was awarded to Rufus Johnson of Mapleton. Salvaging the lumber was no small feat. The house was built with square nails, which have such a small head they are impossible to pull out. After much effort Johnson salvaged the lumber and used it to build a store in Mapleton.

Shortly after the dismantling of the head keeper's house, the United States entered into World War II. The surprise attack on Pearl Harbor put residents along the Oregon Coast in constant fear of attack. Where the head keeper's house once stood, temporary barracks were erected to house about 70 men in the Coast Guard Beach Patrol. Day and night the soldiers patrolled the beaches and headlands from Florence to Yachats with attack dogs, watching for Japanese landing parties. At the lighthouse a small observation shack equipped with a radio was staffed around the clock with orders to watch for Japanese submarines. The duplex's windows were covered in black to keep light from escaping. The lighthouse was so important for the navigation of U.S. war and merchant ships, however, that the light was allowed to shine out to sea. Citizens were told to plant Victory Gardens to conserve resources. Above what currently are the Sea Lion Caves, the Coast Guard planted gardens as instructed. The public was prohibited from visiting Heceta Head during the time it served as a military base. An armed sentry was stationed at the end of the driveway to ensure compliance.

After the end of the war the Coast Guard continued to operate Heceta Head. Cap Herman retired in 1950 after serving 49 distinguished years as light keeper. The 1950s were quiet times at Heceta Head. Oswald Allik, the last civilian light keeper to tend Heceta Head, arrived in 1957 after turning off the light at Tillamook Rock Lighthouse. In 1963 the Coast Guard, once again looking for ways to save money, decided to automate the lighthouse and Allik was instructed to prepare Heceta Head. That summer a sensor was placed in the lighthouse that would alert the Coast Guard if anything were amiss.

The era of the light keepers passed quickly. In just 29 years the lighthouse went from an oil lamp to an automated computer system. Since there was no need to staff the lighthouse, the Coast Guard soon gave the duplex and the land around it to the U.S. Forest Service. The tower and oil houses were given to the Oregon Parks and Recreation Department, yet until 2001 the lens and mechanisms were monitored and maintained by the Coast Guard's Aide to Navigation Team.

For five years the U.S. Forest Service debated the fate of the duplex. Some forest service personnel became tenants; since these families had full-time jobs at other locations, maintenance of the house with its demanding schedule rapidly declined. As the conditions deteriorated public interest escalated, and Friends of Heceta House became a public forum creating guidelines for its next purpose. Lane Community College jumped in with the idea of an offsite campus. Teachers would be able to take their classes, be it watercolors, creative writing, or biology, to Heceta House for several days of intensive study. Boys bunked in the west duplex and girls in the east, bathrooms were installed, and a kitchen was altered for the dormlike use. The college agreed to regular interior maintenance and to hiring a full-time caretaker. However, because the dining room wall was removed to allow a larger space for teaching, the building lost its status as a duplex. Restoration was not an element in the interior work during those 20 years, but it was kept to livable standards and sidestepped many notions of demolition.

In 1978 the duplex was placed on the National Register of Historic Places, assuring continued rehabilitation and restoration efforts. After many studies, surveys of the existing structures, and the clever acquisition of funding, a team of architects was given the task of restoring the exterior. In the early 1980s, it underwent major renovations. The picket fence and front porch were rebuilt, and the half-moon windows, the roof, and fine architectural adornments were replaced. Loyd Collett pioneered these efforts; his photography depicting before-and-after restoration highlights the grandeur of the project.

As the Forest Service gained momentum with exterior rehabilitation, talk arose for undertaking the interior as well. The college had met its end of the bargain but was limited in funding. The Forest Service started exploring alternative uses that would provide funding for the entire structure and broaden its historic elements and public involvement so public tours of the house could be available. But what would allow that to happen? The idea of a bed and breakfast was born. The duplex would return to the status of a home, a home with period antiques and interpretive pieces that would tell its rich history. It would create income for the forest service that would in turn be used to maintain the duplex.

People would be given an opportunity to share in the living history and stay the night in one of the last remaining keeper's dwellings on the West Coast. Finally and most important, it would be open during summer for interpretive tours.

In 1995 the college vacated and inside renovations began with volunteers giving their expertise and time to the project. The walls were painted and rooms furnished in preparation for opening as a bed and breakfast. Mike and Carol Korgan, executive chefs and owners of Korgan's Strudel House in Portland, were chosen as the first innkeepers and agreed to volunteer their time for one year. During one of the roughest winter storms in recent history, the Korgans moved in their belongings. Luckily, they had a passion for antiques and a good eye for them too. Every piece from the moving van seemed to settle in nicely; each piece moved brought them one step closer to turning the duplex back into a home. For Carol it was kind of like returning to her childhood farm. They soon had chickens, two goats, two cats, lots of rabbits, and a little dachshund. Historic tours began and visitors were ecstatic to finally see the inside of this mysterious place.

With such instant success, the Forest Service urged Mike and Carol to stay another five years to run the business and maintain the house. During that time their daughter, Michelle, and her husband, Steven, joined their efforts and as a family continued to improve the duplex and grounds. As the five years passed, many accomplishments were achieved—such as a thriving interpretive center with thousands of visitors every year, a state-of-the-art interior sprinkler system and alarm system, and many restoration and rehabilitation projects for the entire duplex. Though Michelle and Steven had just begun, Carol and Mike were ready to retire again. After a public bid and eager planning with the Forest Service, Michelle and Steven agreed to keep the torch burning for many years to come. Today they work closely with the forest service, striving to make the duplex "five stars" in lightstation terms. These goals are met by the hard work of a dedicated staff and dozens of loyal volunteers. They will help the lighthouse shine for decades to come.

Written by Steven Bursey

FRUIT

AFTER WE SERVE A CUP of our Heceta Head Blend coffee or an Oregon tea blend, fresh fruit seems a natural way to begin our seven courses. Fruit stimulates the appetite and the mind. The first course fruit is always fresh to open the palate, and the spike of sugar gets the conversation rolling. We created these dishes to say "good morning" with every bite.

Careful shopping is half the work for the fruit course. Starting in Yachats and extending east to the Willamette Valley and then beyond, we find the best quality organically grown fruits. We make connections with fruit growers and buy from them yearly, patiently waiting for the next season just as the  last ripe fruit has been consumed. Then we visit local farms and farmers' markets in search of the perfect fruit. It is not unheard of for us to pick each fruit by hand. Looking over, feeling, and smelling the fruit is the only way to guarantee quality. Some kinds of fruit, such as pears, are not fully ripe when purchased; this is okay—and preferable. All winter long we keep them cool and ripen them as needed. Different fruit ripens in different conditions and at different speeds, so it is worth the time to learn how to handle each kind to help achieve optimum flavor.

Having traveled to Hawaii, Mexico, and extensively throughout Southeast Asia, we have had the pleasure of experiencing sweet, sometimes even perfumey, tropical fruits. Some of the following recipes are inspired by those visits; unfortunately, we haven't yet figured out how to grow pineapple in the Northwest! We consider these imports a delicacy, a blessing not taken for granted. In the winter we savor fresh citrus from California and papaya from Mexico and Hawaii. What a wonderful time to be alive when the local food movement is strong and the global environment allows us to splurge on a mango.

FRUIT PLATE

The fruit plate should have variety of options that complement one another in taste, color, and texture. Choose what is the most ripe for the season in your area. If you do not have a lot available, don't give up. Many grocers will be happy to order produce for enthusiastic foodies, especially if you get your friends to buy some as well. At the breakfast table we try to have one or two unusual fruits so our guests can experiment and talk about them.

When we shop for fruit, we take note of the variety and the farm we purchased it from so we can share it with our guests. If there is a limited supply, we may just suggest the general area. It is a big temptation to covet really good fruit!

Fruit is the first course and is prepared about a half hour before breakfast. If you would like to highlight apples and pears, cut them at the last minute and dunk them in an ice water bath with a touch of lemon juice to keep them from turning brown.

White Chocolate Frangelico Cream
(recipe follows)

FRUIT IDEAS:

Berries: blueberry, strawberry, raspberry, marionberry, loganberry, blackberry, tayberry

Cherries: Bing or Rainier

Citrus: navel orange, blood orange, grapefruit, pomelo, tangerine, mandarin, cumquat (Except for the cumquat, remove the rind and as many seeds as possible from the citrus.)

Melons: Crenshaw, canary, Galia, cantaloupe, honeydew, watermelon

Pitted fruits: apricot, nectarine, plum, pluot, fresh prunes

Tropical fruits: papaya, mango, Asian pear, pineapple, star fruit (carambola), custard apple (cherimoya), kiwi fruit

Fresh fig, mini-banana, champagne grapes, Fuyu persimmon

Prepare the cream and refrigerate until ready to use.

Cut each fruit into different shapes and pieces. Do not make the pieces too big; your guests will want a variety to choose from without getting full on fruit alone. Remove rinds and seeds so guests can enjoy the fruit without peeling and seeding. The most impressive part about this dish besides the high quality of the fruit is the display. Have fun layering the fruit on a large decorative plate so that when finished it looks like an exotic flower or a kaleidoscope image. It does take some practice and patience, but it's worth it!

If your platter is large enough, put the cream in a pretty bowl in the middle and build your fruit creation around it. If not, pass the cream on a separate plate with its own spoon.

White Chocolate Frangelico Cream

Chop the chocolate into thin chunks using a large chef's knife and place in a mixing bowl. In a heavy saucepan, bring the cream just to a boil. When it starts to boil it will start to rise very rapidly. Take it off the burner and pour it over the chocolate. Let it stand for 5 minutes. With a whisk mix the chocolate and cream thoroughly. Add the liqueur, mix again and bring to room temperature, about 1 hour. Cover and chill until ready to serve.

4 ounces white chocolate

1 cup heavy cream (see page 181)

1 shot Frangelico liqueur

Makes about 1 ½ cups.

MOROCCAN FRUIT SALAD

2 teaspoons local wildflower honey
(see page 182)

⅓ cup plain whole milk yogurt

1 Fuji apple

1 Bartlett pear

1 banana

4 fresh mint leaves plus 6 sprigs, for
garnish

½ teaspoon orange flower water
(see page 183)

⅓ cup pomegranate seeds,
cherries, or strawberries, for garnish

This salad is one of our favorites because it is so refreshing. It blends the harvest of the Northwest with the exotic flavors of the Middle East. Many of the ingredients may be available to you locally. There is nothing like fresh local honey, and today there are many varieties to choose from. This is a perfect holiday dish with the hints of red and green in this predominantly white dish. But we make this dish all year-round, replacing the pomegranate with cherries and the pears with mango.

In a small bowl, mix the honey and yogurt until the honey is completely incorporated with the yogurt. Set aside.

Quarter, core, peel, and cut the apple and pear into ½-inch pieces. Peel and cut the banana into ½-inch pieces. You don't want the pieces to be so small that the mixture becomes a relish, but there should be no more than a bit of apple, pear, and banana in each bite. Mince the mint leaves.

Gently mix the fruit, mint, and flower water in a bowl. Carefully fold the yogurt mixture into the fruit until the fruit is well coated. Serve in individual dishes or compotes and top each with pomegranate seeds and a sprig of fresh mint.

Makes about six ⅓-cup servings.

Citrus Salad with Ginger Crème Fraîche

Winter is a perfect time for this salad, with the abundance of ripe and succulent citrus fruits available. Choose a complementary variety.

To peel the ginger, scrape it with the tip of a spoon. With a fine grater, shave the ginger and add it to the crème fraîche. Stir in the sugar and set aside.

Zest (see page 184) several curls from each fruit before removing the rind. To remove the rinds, put the citrus on a cutting board and hold it steady with one hand on top of the fruit. Starting from the top and moving down, carve just between the rind and the fruit. Rotate the fruit as each strip of peel is removed until the citrus is completely peeled.

To section the fruit, cut in between the membrane that separates each section. Cut on both sides of the membrane to the center of the fruit; each section should pop out. Try not to let the sections break. (After removing all the sections, squeeze the fruit of its remaining juice and drink it!) Some citrus has very thin sections and would be too difficult to section this way. Therefore, after you cut off the rind, thinly slice the citrus into rounds and then perhaps quarter them.

Lay out small plates. To serve, start with the largest wedges and place them in a circle around each plate's edge. Face them in the same direction with the points in the middle coming in toward each other. Descend in size so you fill in the gaps between the larger pieces, eventually ending with the smallest piece. You'll see a flower shape emerge. Arrange any fruit cut into quarters in the middle of the plate. Spoon a small dollop of the crème fraîche mixture in the center. Accent the center with the reserved zest curls. Serve a small plate to each guest.

Makes 6 small plates.

1 1-inch piece fresh ginger

½ cup crème fraîche (see page 176)

4 teaspoons sugar

1 pomelo or ugli fruit

1 ruby red grapefruit

1 blood orange

2 honey tangerines

TROPICAL FRUIT SALAD

In the middle of winter during a dramatic storm there is nothing like the sunny taste of tropical fruit. Considering how rough it was to live at the lighthouse 100 years ago, this salad celebrates the Million Dollar Mile, Highway 101.

These are the fruits we usually use, but like with many of our recipes, the best fruits to use are the freshest, ripest, most seasonal available. Have fun choosing yours.

½ lime

¼ cup sweetened condensed milk

¼ cup coconut powder (see page 181)

1 tablespoon water

¼ honeydew, Crenshaw, or other pale melon

½ mango

1 kiwi fruit

¼ pineapple

½ Hawaiian papaya or ¼ small Mexican papaya

Squeeze the juice from the lime and reserve the rind. In a small dish, mix the condensed milk, coconut powder, water, and 1½ teaspoons of the lime juice and set aside.

Seed the melon with a spoon. Remove the rind from the melon, mango, pineapple, and kiwi fruit. Remove the core from the pineapple. Except the papaya, cut all the fruits to about the size of a nickel and about ½ inch thick. (Any smaller and the salad will be more like a relish and the ripe fruits can easily start to break down. If the pieces are larger, guests lose the ability to have a few fruits in each bite.) Gently mix the fruit and spoon them into pretty individual glasses. Spoon the condensed milk mixture over each.

Seed the papaya, remove the rind, and cut the papaya lengthwise into thin spears. Pour the remaining lime juice over the spears to coat. Place them on top of the fruit-filled glasses to form a bird of paradise look. Julienne the lime peel into one-pointed spears and use them to accent the papaya.

Makes about six ⅓-cup servings.

PINOT GRIS COCKTAIL

Pinot Gris has crisp citrus and honey notes that blend well with fresh fruit. And with mascarpone and candied nuts: heaven. Impress your guests with a local wine. If Pinot Gris is not available, other white wines without oak will work. Pay attention to the sugar content of the wine and adjust the recipe accordingly so it is not too sweet.

Prepare and cool the syrup and add the cantaloupe and pear the day before serving.

Wine Simple Syrup (recipe follows)

⅓ cantaloupe, rind removed

1 Asian pear

1 pint strawberries

½ small or personal watermelon or about 2 cups, rind removed

Mascarpone cream (recipe follows)

Candied hazelnuts (recipe follows)

Cut the cantaloupe into nickel-size triangular pieces and the pear into ⅓-inch cubes. Mix in a container with a lid and pour the wine syrup over the fruit. Cover and refrigerate overnight.

Wash and hull the strawberries. About 30 minutes before serving, cut them into spears and the watermelon into ½-inch cubes. Add the strawberries and watermelon to the other fruit and syrup. Mix and set aside.

To serve, use a slotted spoon to drain excess syrup and place the wine-soaked fruit into individual glasses. Add extra syrup if desired. Spoon the mascarpone cream over the fruit and sprinkle with the nuts.

Makes 2 cups or 6 small servings.

⅓ cup sugar

1 cup Pinot Gris

Wine Simple Syrup

In a heavy saucepan on medium-low heat, melt the sugar in the wine. When the sugar is completely dissolved, remove the pan from the heat and let cool.

Makes 1⅓ cups.

⅓ cup mascarpone (see page 182)

2 tablespoons heavy cream (see page 181)

Mascarpone Cream

Whip the mascarpone and cream until smooth and fluffy. Add a little extra cream if the mixture seems too thick. Do not overmix or it may turn to butter.

Makes a heaping ⅓ cup.

Candied Hazelnuts

1 cup roasted hazelnuts

½ cup brown sugar

2 teaspoons butter

Chop the nuts roughly into quarters. In a nonstick pan, heat the nuts and brown sugar on medium high until the sugar starts to melt. Stir constantly while periodically removing the pan from the heat to avoid burning. Do not let the mixture smoke. When the sugar glistens and coats the nuts, remove from the heat and add the butter to coat. Spread the nuts on tinfoil and let cool. Crumble and keep in an airtight container up to 2 weeks or freeze up to 2 months.

Makes about 1½ cups.

OREGON BERRIES WITH ELDERBERRY SYRUP
AND HEAVY CREAM

In Oregon we are blessed with an abundance of wild and cultivated berries. We have even come up with our own berry, the marionberry. Developed at Oregon State University, the marionberry is a cross between the Chehalem blackberry and the olallieberry. It was designed so that it can freeze well and still maintain its structure after thawing—and to make the tastiest berry imaginable.

Berries and cream are a classic combination that has no parallel when berries are at the peak of their ripeness. We usually combine two to four berries or some peaches or nectarines when in season. Heavy cream has up to 40 percent fat and is a true luxury. If your grocer does not carry it, whipping cream, although lighter, is acceptable. Most important is freshness—and a locally and organically produced product whenever possible.

Elderflower syrup is available through specialty food stores. It has a unique, slightly floral and earthy taste that when blended with the lemon thyme adds another dimension to this simple classic dish.

3 cups berries
(combination of any two to four):
strawberries, blueberries,
marionberries, raspberries, tayberries,
boysenberries, blackberries

2 tablespoons elderflower syrup
(see page 181)

1 cup heavy cream (see page 181)

6 sprigs lemon thyme, optional

Wash, hull, and slice the strawberries, if using. Rinse the blueberries, if using, in a strainer and set aside to drip-dry. If you are using other unsprayed cultivated berries that look clean and not dusty, you needn't wash them, especially raspberries. Washing berries tends to waterlog them and break their delicate skins. If you must rinse them, do it gently with a fine spray and serve within 1 or 2 hours.

Place all the berries in a bowl. Drizzle the syrup over the fruit and gently mix, being careful not to smash the berries.

To serve, place the berries in attractive individual dishes with room enough for the cream. Garnish each with a sprig of the lemon thyme. Pass the cream so guests may choose to have cream or just enjoy the berries by themselves.

When I add cream to the fruit, I later find that the best part is the cream at the bottom that has collected all the wonderful berry flavor. A nibble on the lemon thyme will enhance the flavor combination and cleanse your palate after having the rich cream.

Makes about 3 cups or 6 small servings.

ANISE HONEY DRESSING WITH PITTED FRUITS

Like fennel, anise is one of those flavors people love or love to hate. We feel one of the most gratifying things about cooking is changing a person's negative opinion about certain foods. Countless times at the breakfast table we overhear, "Oh, I thought I didn't like this dish or that flavor." Or, "I have never tried this because I assumed I wouldn't like it. This is really wonderful, mmmm." If you listen closely after hearing comments like these, you may hear a victory "Yes!" coming from the kitchen.

The anise in this recipe is really mild and pairs nicely with the tannic skins of plums and nectarines. Sneak it to a friend who doesn't usually care for anise; it will most likely be a pleasant surprise. (Please be discerning; there is a difference between dislike and allergy.)

Dressing (recipe follows)

3 plums

3 apricots

2 nectarines

Edible flowers such as pansies, borage flowers, or nasturtiums, for garnish

Prepare the dressing and set aside.

Slice the fruits from their pits and arrange on individual plates in fan shapes or other decorative fashion. Drizzle the dressing over the fruit and decorate with edible flowers.

Makes about 3 cups or 6 small servings.

½ teaspoon ground anise

½ teaspoon dry mustard

½ teaspoon paprika

Pinch salt

¼ cup fireweed or other local honey (see page 182)

1 tablespoon lemon juice

1 tablespoon apple cider vinegar

¼ cup vegetable oil

Dressing
Whisk together the anise, mustard, paprika, salt, honey, lemon juice, and vinegar. Slowly add the oil while whisking to emulsify the dressing. (You can also prepare the dressing in a small food processor.) Set aside.

Makes about ¾ cup.

YOGI TEA FRUIT CUP

This loose tea originated in the Himalayas and has become the base for many tea blends and chai drinks. The main ingredients are cinnamon bark, ginger, clove, black pepper, and cardamom. We recommend you use this original blend without additional ingredients. Ask your local health food store or herbalist for the original blend.

The fruit syrup complements many fruits, but they may not all be ripe at the same time. In the summer we use peaches, strawberries, and Asian pears. In the fall we switch to Fuyu persimmons, Bartlett pears, and fresh figs. In the winter we soak dates in the syrup and serve it with Honeycrisp apples, Comice pears, and blood oranges. Here is a variation for fall to get you started.

Prepare and cool the syrup many hours or overnight before preparing the fruit dish.

Wash and cut the persimmon in ¼-inch rounds, then into eighths, like a pie. Quarter, peel, and core the pear. Cut into ½-inch pieces. Rinse and cut the figs lengthwise into sixths. Mix all the fruits in a bowl. Drizzle the syrup over the fruits and let stand 20 minutes.

To serve, pile the fruits into individual cups. Spoon about 2 teaspoons of crème fraîche over the fruit and sprinkle with the sugar.

Makes 6 small servings.

1 Fuyu persimmon

1 Bartlett pear

6 fresh Celeste or Mission figs

Yogi Syrup (recipe follows)

2 tablespoons crème fraîche (see page 176)

Dark palm sugar or brown sugar for sprinkling

Yogi Syrup

Boil the water and add the loose tea. Remove from the heat and steep for 20 minutes to 1 hour. Strain out the leaves with a fine-mesh strainer and discard.

Mix the tea with the sugar. Return the tea to medium-high heat and dissolve the sugar completely. Set aside to cool; refrigerate until well chilled.

Makes about 2 cups.

1½ cups water

1 tablespoon Yogi tea

½ cup sugar

Watermelon Bouquet

The fresh and sweet fragrance of a good watermelon combined with a hint of rose water, fresh mint, and honey is intoxicating and just the right arrangement for a summer morning or afternoon. If you don't eat it all or if you make extra, it's wonderful with a touch of rum or vodka and a little soda water.

¼ medium watermelon

½ teaspoon finely chopped fresh mint

½ teaspoon rose water (see page 183)

2 teaspoons wildflower honey (see page 182)

Rose petals and fresh mint, for garnish

Remove the rind from the watermelon. Cut the melon into ½-inch slices and again into thirds, cutting the chunks at an angle back and forth to make triangles about ½ inch thick and the widest no more then 2 inches. Place in a mixing bowl; sprinkle the chopped mint over the watermelon but do not mix.

In a small bowl mix the rose water and honey, then drizzle over the watermelon and gently fold it in with the mint.

To serve, spoon into individual serving glasses and top with a rose petal and sprig of fresh mint.

Makes 6 small servings.

SWEET BREAD

WE SERVE THESE BREADS TO complement the fruit course. Some of our favorite combinations are Moroccan Fruit Salad with Sailor Bread, Oregon Berries with Elderberry Syrup and Heavy Cream with Carol's Orange Bread, Citrus Salad with Heceta Bright Bread, and Oregon Pinot Gris Cocktail with Sublime Banana Bread with Oregon Hazelnut Praline. In addition, these breads go very well with afternoon tea or coffee.

All recipes make three loaves so you can freeze a couple or share them with friends. At the B&B we make six at a time and freeze them. We use one loaf every day so they are frozen for no more than a week or so, but freezing them actually makes them moister! Before freezing make sure they are completely cool or they can become crumbly. The day before serving, take a loaf out of the freezer and let it thaw in the refrigerator. Thirty minutes before serving, slice the loaf about ½ inch thick, and keeping the loaf together put it on the serving plate. Cover the loaf with foil and put it in a warmer or very low oven. When you serve it, make sure the plate is cool enough for your guests to pass.

CAROL'S ORANGE BREAD

While vacationing in Honolulu, Mike and Carol were told to go to Stewart's Drug Store for breakfast because the locals raved about the store's orange bread. Curious Carol (an infamous collector of menus!) asked for the recipe, but she could get just the ingredients, not the proportions. Carol figured out the proportions, and Mike liked her orange bread even better. Stewart's Drug Store may be long gone, but the orange bread lives on.

4 cups all-purpose flour

1½ cups plus 2 tablespoons sugar, divided

1½ teaspoons salt

2 tablespoons baking powder

1 orange including rind, quartered and seeds removed

Orange juice, if needed

2 large eggs

½ cup canola oil

1½ teaspoons vanilla extract

1½ cups whole milk

Preheat the oven to 400°F and oil three 8-by-4-inch bread pans with baking spray.

Sift the flour, 1½ cups of the sugar, salt, and baking powder together and set aside.

In a small food processor, puree the orange to make 1 cup. If necessary, add enough orange juice to make 1 cup. Set aside.

In a large bowl, beat the eggs thoroughly. Add the oil in a slow, steady stream. Beat for 1 minute. Add the puree and vanilla. Add the dry ingredients, alternating with the milk, starting and ending with the dry ingredients.

Divide the batter evenly among the pans. Sprinkle with the remaining 2 tablespoons of sugar. Let the batter sit for 20 minutes before baking. Place the pans on a baking sheet and bake 15 minutes. With a sharp knife, score the tops down the middle lengthwise (which keeps the bread from splitting on the sides and overflowing). Reduce the temperature to 325°F and bake for another 40 minutes or until a toothpick inserted in the center of 2 loaves comes out clean. Let cool in the pans for 20 minutes; turn out and let rest on a wire rack until cool. See page 47 for storing breads.

Makes 3 loaves.

SAILOR'S BREAD

This bread contains no dairy or eggs. Make the loaves for your vegan friends; they'll be grateful and impressed. Legend has it this bread was made during long voyages when eggs and butter were scarce but spices were aplenty. Arrgh, and a little rum never hurt anyone!

Begin this recipe the day before baking.

Combine 2 cups of the sugar, cocoa, cinnamon, nutmeg, allspice, cloves, and salt in a medium saucepan. Add 2 cups of the water, rum, and raisins. Simmer over medium heat until hot but not boiling; remove from the heat. Cover the mixture and let stand at room temperature overnight.

The next day preheat the oven to 350°F and oil three 8-by-4-inch bread pans with baking spray.

Add the oil, the remaining ½ cup of water, and honey to the cocoa mixture.

In a large mixing bowl, sift the flour, cake flour, baking soda, and baking powder together three times. Add the cocoa mixture and mix until combined.

Divide the mixture among the pans and sprinkle with the remaining 2 tablespoons of sugar. Place the pans on a baking sheet and bake for 60 minutes or until a toothpick inserted in the center of 2 breads comes out clean. Let cool for 30 minutes; turn out and let rest on a wire rack until completely cool. See page 47 for storing the breads.

Makes 3 loaves.

2 cups plus 2 tablespoons sugar, divided

¼ cup cocoa

1 tablespoon ground cinnamon

1½ teaspoons freshly ground nutmeg

1 teaspoon ground allspice

1 teaspoon ground cloves

2 teaspoons salt

2 cups plus ½ cup water, divided

¼ cup spiced rum

1 cup raisins

1⅔ cups vegetable oil

3 tablespoons honey

2½ cups all-purpose flour

2½ cups cake flour

3 teaspoons baking soda

1½ teaspoons baking powder

HECETA BRIGHT BREAD

*Michelle created this bread on one of those Oregon Coast winter days—
she wanted to brighten things up and serve something full of surprises. The
ingredients and their colors not only look nice but taste wonderful as well.*

4 cups all-purpose flour

1 tablespoon baking powder

1 teaspoon baking soda

1 teaspoon salt

½ cup dried cranberries

¾ cup dried apricots

3 small chunks candied ginger
(see page 181)

4 large eggs

2 cups grated small unpeeled zucchini

¾ cup plus 2 tablespoons sugar, divided

¾ cup brown sugar

¾ cup vegetable oil

4 tablespoons lemon juice (see Note)

2 teaspoons lemon zest
(see Note; see page 184)

Preheat the oven to 350°F and oil three 8-by-4-inch bread pans with
baking spray.

Sift the flour, baking powder, baking soda, and salt together. Set aside.

Chop the cranberries, apricots, and candied ginger into small bits (pea
size or smaller) and set aside.

In a large mixing bowl beat the eggs until foamy. Add ¾ cup of the sugar
and the brown sugar, beating thoroughly. Add the oil in a slow stream
and mix well. Add the lemon juice and zest. Add half the flour mixture.
Stop to scrape down the sides and the bottom. Add the remaining flour
and mix just to combine. Gently fold in the zucchini and cranberry mixture with a wooden spoon.

Divide the batter among the pans and sprinkle with the remaining
2 tablespoons of sugar. Place the pans on a baking sheet and bake for
55 minutes or until a toothpick inserted in the center of 2 breads comes
out clean. Let rest for 20 minutes; turn out and let rest on a wire rack
until completely cool. See page 47 for storing the breads.

Note: One lemon will yield about 2 tablespoons of zest and 4 tablespoons of juice.

Makes 3 loaves.

BROWNIE'S RARE AND FAMOUS CRANBERRY BREAD

This recipe is from Michelle's sister-in-law's grandmother Brownie. It's been said she was as sweet, nutty, and zesty as the bread. Thanks for the recipe, Brownie!

4 cups fresh or frozen cranberries

4 cups all-purpose flour

3 teaspoons baking powder

1 teaspoon baking soda

1 teaspoon salt

1½ cups unsalted butter

3 cups sugar

3 large eggs

Zest from 2 oranges (see page 184)

1½ cups hazelnuts, walnuts, or pecans, finely chopped

Preheat the oven to 350°F and oil three 8-by-4-inch bread pans with baking spray.

In a food processor pulse cranberries until they are fairly minced but not pasty. Set aside.

Sift the flour, baking powder, baking soda, and salt together. Set aside.

Cream the butter until light. Add the sugar and beat until fluffy. Add the eggs one at a time until well mixed. Scrape down the sides and bottom and mix again. Add the zest. Add the dry ingredients and mix just to blend. Mix in the cranberries and nuts. If you are using a mixer, it will be easier to add the cranberries and nuts by hand because the batter will be very thick.

Divide the batter among the pans. Place the pans on a baking sheet and bake for about 1 hour, turning the pans at 30 minutes and checking at 50 minutes. Breads are done when a toothpick inserted in the center of 2 breads comes out clean. Let rest for 20 minutes; turn out and let rest on a wire rack until completely cool. See page 47 for storing the breads.

Makes 3 loaves.

Sweet Cardamom Tomato Bread

It may sound a little unusual, but sweet tomatoes are really good in bread. The cardamom adds depth and spice. It is fine to use canned tomatoes if they are good quality. If you use fresh tomatoes, choose only vine ripened ones. Peel and dice them.

Preheat the oven to 350°F and oil three 8-by-4-inch bread pans. In a mixing bowl sift the flour, baking soda, baking powder, and cardamom together. Set aside.

Place the tomatoes and juice in a small food processor. Pulse just to chop, but do not puree.

Beat the eggs in a mixer. Add 1½ cups of the sugar and the oil and mix until well blended. Add the vanilla, tomatoes, and catsup and mix. Fold into the flour mixture and mix only until moist. Divide the batter among the pans and sprinkle with the remaining sugar.

Place the pans on a baking sheet and bake for 60 minutes, checking at 50 minutes for doneness. Breads are done when a toothpick inserted in the center of 2 loaves comes out clean. Let rest for 20 minutes; turn out and let rest on a wire rack until cool. See page 47 for storing the breads.

Makes 3 loaves.

4 cups all-purpose flour

1 teaspoon baking soda

½ teaspoon baking powder

2 teaspoons ground cardamom

1⅔ cups peeled and chopped tomatoes, with juice

3 large eggs

1½ cups sugar, plus additional for sprinkling

1 cup vegetable oil

1 teaspoon vanilla extract

⅓ cup catsup

Date Pine Nut Citron Bread

Citron is a candied fruit most widely known as an ingredient in fruit cakes. Unlike other citrus citron is not consumed in its natural state but is first brined and candied. It lends a mild citrus taste to the bread and complements the richness of the dates and pine nuts. This is one of our favorite winter breads.

2 teaspoons baking soda

2 cups boiling water

1 pound pitted Medjool dates, diced

3 cups all-purpose flour

3 tablespoons unsalted butter

2 cups plus 2 tablespoons sugar, divided

3 large eggs

1 teaspoon vanilla extract

1 teaspoon salt

1 cup whole pine nuts

⅓ cup citron

Dissolve the baking soda in boiling water and pour it over the dates. Set aside for 1 hour.

Preheat the oven to 325°F and oil three 8-by-4-inch pans with baking spray. Set aside. Sift the flour and set aside.

In a mixer cream the butter and 2 cups of the sugar. Add the eggs, vanilla, and salt. Add the dates and mix on low speed to break them up. Add the flour; scrape down the sides and bottom of the bowl. Add the pine nuts and citron just to combine.

Divide the batter among the pans and sprinkle with the remaining 2 tablespoons of sugar. Place the pans on a baking sheet and bake for 1 hour and 15 minutes. Check for doneness. Breads are done when a toothpick inserted in the center of 2 loaves comes out clean. Let rest for 20 minutes; turn out and let rest on a wire rack until completely cool. See page 47 for storing the breads.

Makes 3 loaves.

TRIPLE GINGERBREAD

Sometimes the best recipes are born from mistakes. Carol started making gingerbread and found she had no ground ginger. She searched her pantry and found candied ginger, and in the fridge, fresh ginger. Thinking the fresh ginger would not be potent enough, she chopped the candied ginger and added it as well. Oh, the bread was good! The next time she made ginger-bread she had ground ginger but still added fresh and candied ginger— still not too much! Three kinds of ginger are best.

In a small saucepan over low heat, heat the butter, brown sugar, and molasses. Mix until the butter melts and the sugar is dissolved. Stir in the raisins and set aside to cool.

Preheat the oven to 400°F and oil three 8-by-4-inch bread pans with baking spray. Sift the flour, baking soda, salt, cinnamon, mace, cloves, mustard, pepper, and ground ginger together. Set aside.

In a mixing bowl, beat the eggs and add the buttermilk. Be certain the molasses mixture is cool; then add to the egg mixture. Add the candied and fresh ginger. Add the dry ingredients and stir only to combine. Divide the mixture among the prepared pans. Sprinkle with the sugar and place the pans on a baking sheet.

Bake for 15 minutes. Reduce the oven temperature to 350°F and bake for 45 minutes. Breads are done when a toothpick inserted in the center of 2 loaves comes out clean. Let rest for 20 minutes; turn out and let rest on a wire rack until cool. See page 47 for storing the breads.

Makes 3 loaves.

1 cup unsalted butter

1 cup brown sugar

1 cup molasses

½ cup golden raisins

4 cups all-purpose flour

2 teaspoons baking soda

1 teaspoon salt

2 teaspoons ground cinnamon

½ teaspoon mace

½ teaspoon ground cloves

1 teaspoon dry mustard

1 teaspoon black pepper

1 tablespoon ground ginger

2 large eggs

1 cup buttermilk

½ cup candied ginger, finely chopped (see page 181)

2 teaspoons finely chopped fresh ginger

2 tablespoons sugar for sprinkling

RASPBERRY BREAD

After Carol's mother, Marie, passed away, Carol found this recipe with a note that said, "Michelle really liked these." Considering Marie had more than 50 grandchildren, it was nice to know she welcomed her granddaughter's opinion.

This bread has become a favorite at the B&B. If fresh raspberries are out of season, use individually frozen raspberries. During berry season we put up as many berries as possible to get us through the winter months. See page 177 on how to freeze berries.

Preheat the oven to 350°F and oil three 8-by-4-inch baking pans with baking spray. Pick through the raspberries and gently wash them with a fine spray. Set aside in a strainer to dry. If you use frozen berries, do not let them thaw. Take them out of the freezer just when you need them. (They should already be washed.)

Sift the flour, baking powder, and salt together. Set aside.

In a mixer cream the butter and 2 cups of the sugar until light. Add the eggs one at a time, beating well after each addition. Mix thoroughly; scrape down the sides and bottom of the bowl. Starting and ending with the dry ingredients, add them alternately with the milk. Fold in the berries. Divide the batter evenly among the pans. Sprinkle with the remaining 2 tablespoons of sugar.

Place the pans on a baking sheet and bake for 55 to 60 minutes. Check for doneness. If you used frozen berries, you may need 5 to 7 minutes more baking time. Breads are done when a toothpick inserted in the center of 2 loaves comes out clean. Let rest for 30 minutes. To remove from the pans, run a knife around the edges to separate any berries that may be stuck to the sides. Turn out and let rest on a wire rack until completely cool. See page 47 for storing the breads.

Makes 3 loaves.

2 cups fresh raspberries

4 cups all-purpose flour

4 teaspoons baking powder

1 teaspoon salt

1 cup unsalted butter

2 cups plus 2 tablespoons sugar, divided

4 large eggs

1 cup whole milk

SUBLIME BANANA BREAD WITH
OREGON HAZELNUT PRALINE

Banana bread recipes are always best when they come from little old ladies. After a wild-edibles course on San Juan Island, Michelle visited a friend in Friday Harbor. While Michelle sat at the local watering hole where her friend tended bar, a regular happy hour patron came in with this bread. Enamored by how buttery it was, Michelle asked for the recipe. The sweet and rather tipsy old lady promptly grabbed a cocktail napkin and jotted it down. Michelle's praline topping pushed it over the edge.

6 overripe bananas (about 3 cups)

1 tablespoon lemon juice

2½ cups all-purpose flour

2 teaspoons baking soda

1 teaspoon salt

1 cup unsalted butter

2 cups sugar

4 large eggs, well beaten

Topping (recipe follows)

Preheat the oven to 350°F and oil three 8-by-4-inch bread pans with baking spray. In a small food processor, pulse the banana and lemon juice until the banana is almost smooth.

In a large bowl, sift the flour, baking soda, and salt together three times. Set aside.

Cream the butter and sugar until light and fluffy. Add the bananas and eggs, beating until well mixed. Add to the dry ingredients and stir to blend; do not overmix.

Pour the mixture into the prepared pans; place the pans on a baking sheet and bake for 50 to 60 minutes. Check for doneness. Breads are done when a toothpick inserted in the center of 2 loaves comes out clean. While the bread is cooling in the pans, prepare the topping.

While the topping is still warm, spoon it onto the cooled loaves and spread it. Let rest for 1 to 2 hours; turn out of the pans. See page 47 for storing the breads.

Makes 3 loaves.

½ cup heavy cream (see page 181)

2 tablespoons unsalted butter

½ cup brown sugar

1½ cups roasted hazelnuts, chopped (see page 178)

2 teaspoons vanilla extract

Topping

In a small saucepan over medium heat, heat the cream and butter. Place the brown sugar in another small heavy saucepan over medium-high heat. Stir constantly with a wooden spoon until the sugar is melted. There should be no granules; melted sugar should be smooth and have a slightly darker color. Slowly stir in the cream mixture, making sure it is being incorporated as you pour. If you pour too quickly the cream will clump, making it more difficult to work, so take your time working it in with the wooden spoon.

When all the cream has been added and the mixture is smooth again, remove from the heat and stir in the hazelnuts and vanilla.

FRESH PUMPKIN RUM BREAD

We get the most amazing pumpkins at the Morning Glory Farm in Walton, Oregon. Sandy has so many to choose from and they are all so yummy that it's hard to pick a favorite. The one we used for this recipe was Musque de Provence. It yielded about 14 cups of fresh pumpkin, which is nothing like canned pumpkin. It is ultra-bright, light, and sweet. If you can get local pumpkins for eating, we highly recommend it for any of your pumpkin recipes. See page 178 for instructions on how to roast and puree pumpkin for this recipe and others.

Combine the raisins and rum and set aside to soak. Preheat the oven to 350°F and oil three 8-by-4-inch pans with baking spray.

Sift the flour, baking soda, salt, nutmeg, cinnamon, and ginger together. Set aside.

Beat the eggs in a mixing bowl. Add the brown sugar, sugar, pumpkin, and oil. Scrape down the sides and bottom of the bowl and mix well. With the mixer on low speed, add the dry ingredient and stir only to combine. Stir in the raisin mixture.

Divide the mixture among the pans, put them on a baking sheet, and bake for 50 to 60 minutes. Breads are done when a toothpick inserted in the center of 2 loaves comes out clean. Let rest for 20 minutes; turn out and let rest on a wire rack until completely cool. See page 47 for storing the breads.

Make 3 loaves.

1 cup raisins

½ cup light rum

4 cups all-purpose flour

2 teaspoons baking soda

1 teaspoon salt

1 teaspoon freshly ground nutmeg

1½ teaspoons ground cinnamon

½ teaspoon ground ginger

4 large eggs

1 cup brown sugar

1½ cups sugar

2 cups pumpkin

1 cup vegetable oil

SWEET BASIL BREAD

This is a sweet bread with a kick! Depending on how hot your chili flakes are, you may want to adjust the quantity. We like it spicy. This bread is a perfect combination with the Tropical Fruit Salad (see page 36): a little mango, a little spice. A nice variation is to use Thai basil. It has a very distinct taste and blends well with hot spices. Because Thai basil is so fragrant, use half the amount called for in this recipe.

4 cups all-purpose flour

4 teaspoons baking powder

1 teaspoon salt

1½ teaspoons red chili flakes, ground in a spice mill

2 cups crookneck or yellow squash

6 large eggs

1 cup sugar

2 cups vegetable oil

1 cup chopped fresh basil or ½ cup chopped fresh Thai basil

Preheat the oven to 350°F and oil three 8-by-4-inch pans with baking spray.

Sift together the flour, baking powder, and salt. Stir in the pepper flakes. Set aside.

Grate the squash with the large grate of a box grater. Set aside.

Beat the eggs well in a mixer. Add the sugar and oil. Mix well. Add the sifted ingredients and mix just to combine. Stir in the squash and basil.

Divide the mixture among the pans, put them on a baking sheet, and bake for 50 to 60 minutes. Breads are done when a toothpick inserted in the center of two loaves comes out clean. Let rest for 20 minutes; turn out on a wire rack and let rest until completely cool. See the introduction on page 47 for storing the breads.

Makes 3 loaves.

LEMON POPPY SEED BREAD

This bread is very light in texture and taste. We like to serve it with Oregon Berries with Elderberry Syrup and Heavy Cream (see page 41). It's nice to dunk the bread in the creamy syrup that gathers in the bottom of the dish.

Preheat the oven to 350°F and oil three 8-by-4-inch pans with baking spray. Combine the milk and poppy seed. Set aside.

Sift the flour, 2 cups of the sugar, baking powder, and salt together. Set aside.

In a mixing bowl beat the eggs, oil, zest, and lemon juice. Add the poppy seed mixture. Add the dry ingredients all at once and mix only until combined. Divide the mixture among the pans and sprinkle with the remaining 2 tablespoons of sugar.

Put the pans on a baking sheet and bake for 60 minutes. Breads are done when a toothpick inserted in the center of 2 loaves comes out clean. Let rest for 20 minutes; turn out and let rest on a wire rack until completely cool. See page 47 for storing the breads.

Note: One lemon will yield about 2 tablespoons of zest and 4 tablespoons of juice.

Make 3 loaves.

2 cups whole milk

3 tablespoons poppy seed

4½ cups all-purpose flour

2 cups plus 2 tablespoons sugar, divided

4½ teaspoons baking powder

1½ teaspoons salt

3 large eggs

¾ cup vegetable oil

2 tablespoons lemon zest
(see Note; see page 184)

5 tablespoons lemon juice
(see Note)

MICHELLE'S COCONUT BREAD

Carol has made coconut bread for many years and every time she makes it Michelle tells her, "I like it, but it needs something." So we change this and change that. Michelle recommended adding coconut powder in place of some of the flour. And then we came up with the macaroon topping. After years of experimenting, this bread has become an "ode to the coconut."

Topping (recipe follows)

4 cups all-purpose flour

½ cup coconut powder (see page 181)

2 tablespoons baking powder

1½ teaspoons salt

3 large eggs

1½ cups sugar

1½ teaspoons vanilla extract

1 cup whole milk

1 cup vegetable oil

7 ounces sweetened condensed milk (see Topping recipe)

1½ cups coconut flakes

Preheat the oven to 350°F and oil three 8-by-4-inch pans with baking spray. Sift the flour, coconut powder, baking powder, and salt together. Set aside.

Beat the eggs in a mixer. Add the sugar and beat. Add the vanilla, milk, oil, and condensed milk. Scrape down the sides and bottom of the bowl and mix again. Add the dry ingredients and mix just to combine. Stir in the coconut flakes with a spatula.

Divide the mixture among the pans, put them on a baking sheet, and bake for 50 minutes.

Remove the pans from the oven and quickly top each bread with one-third of the topping. Keep the topping centered so it stays on the top of the bread.

Return the breads to the oven and bake for an additional 5 minutes. Check for doneness. Breads are done when a toothpick inserted in the center of 2 loaves comes out clean. Cool breads completely before removing them from the pans. See page 47 for storing the breads.

Makes 3 loaves.

2 cups coconut flakes

7 ounces sweetened condensed milk (from a 14-ounce can; use the remainder in the bread recipe)

1 teaspoon vanilla extract

¾ teaspoon almond extract

Topping

Mix the coconut flakes, condensed milk, and vanilla and almond extracts; set aside.

SEAFOOD

WHEN WE TELL PEOPLE ABOUT our seven-course breakfast, often they want to know how we break down the courses. And just as often when we tell them the second course is seafood, we get the reply, "Fish for breakfast?" Yes, wonderful fresh Pacific Coast seafood! And when we describe the seafood dishes, we usually hear murmurs of "Mmmm, yum."

At the breakfast table we can use the power of suggestion to create a desire for each dish. We are able to tempt people to try foods they normally would not seek out or foods that they may not like. A favorite response was from a guest who had never tried lox or herring and was pleasantly surprised with both. Our advice to many skeptics is at least once a year try foods they don't like when the food is fresh and well prepared, and especially when they are really hungry. We've been working on Steven with oysters every Christmas Eve and we think it is finally working!

A favorite pastime at Heceta Head is spent at low tide collecting mussels off the rocks. We cook them in dry vermouth, tomatoes, lots of garlic, and fresh parsley and enjoy them with a glass of Pinot Gris and a hunk of bread for dunking.

Safe in our cozy parlor we watch brave men and women working the ocean for our Dungeness crab, wild salmon, and albacore tuna. On the docks in Newport and Florence, we watch them skillfully fillet our fish to order, and within hours it is on our table. Our fisherman friend Jerry swore he could see us during daylight and often told us how thankful he was to see our light at night.

Oregon Lox and Bagels

Nova style lox is salmon that has been lightly brined, cold smoked, and very thinly sliced. When we started the B&B, we tasted lox from all over the country and beyond, searching for the best to serve our guests. We finally found our favorite, made just 70 miles from Heceta Head in Eugene, Oregon. The Oregon Lox Company uses wild Pacific salmon and gently smokes it with alderwood. See Resources, page 185.

Our lox plate is served with cream cheese, toasted mini-bagels, and several garnishes depending on the season. Some favorite choices are finely shaved red or spring onion, slices of yellow and red Roma tomatoes, lemon cucumber, thinly sliced radish, sprigs of baby dill, capers, and freshly ground black pepper.

If you do not have lox available locally, you can have it shipped to you. We also recommend trying any locally smoked fish. We also serve smoked tuna, trout, cod, and halibut.

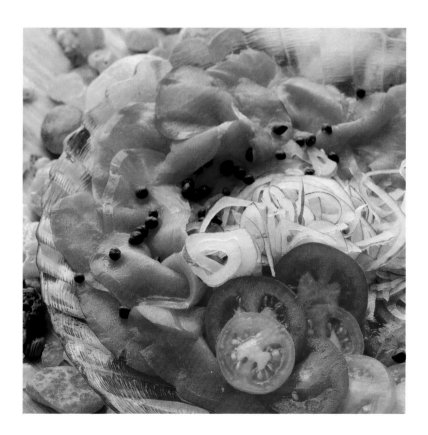

WILD CHINOOK SALMON SWEET CORN CAKES

We make these cakes the day after a salmon barbecue. We grill the salmon over mesquite with dill butter, Walla Walla sweet onion, and lemon. When it has cooled, we refrigerate it, keeping the onion and lemon on top. The next day we have an amazing piece of fish that is wonderful cold with a little aioli (see page 181), and even better in these cakes. They are so good that we always grill extra salmon. What started as a need to use up leftovers has become the reason for the barbecue!

Cucumber cream is an unusual sauce but is a light and refreshing complement to salmon cakes. We whip the cream until it is almost butter. When it's on the salmon cake, it starts to melt like whipped butter on a pancake.

Combine the salmon, corn, and onion. Set aside.

Mix the egg yolks, lemon juice, and mustard. Whisk in the oil and mix well. Add the salt and pepper. Add to the salmon mixture. Add 3 tablespoons of the bread crumbs and mix well.

Place the remaining 1 cup of bread crumbs in a shallow dish. Form about 2 ounces of the salmon mixture into a ball and coat with the bread crumbs. Press the ball into a cake and shake off excess crumbs. Set aside. Repeat, using all the salmon.

Heat the butter in a 12-inch skillet. Add the salmon cakes and cook over medium heat until they are golden brown on each side. Serve immediately with the cucumber cream and a slice of lemon.

Makes 8 cakes.

12 ounces mesquite-grilled wild salmon, flaked

½ cup fresh sweet corn, cooked

2 tablespoons grilled minced onion

3 egg yolks

1 tablespoon lemon juice

3 teaspoons Dijon mustard

2 tablespoons olive oil

¼ teaspoon salt

Freshly ground black pepper

1 cup plus 3 tablespoons fresh bread crumbs, divided (see page 175)

1 tablespoon clarified butter (see page 175)

Cucumber Cream (recipe follows)

Lemon slices, for garnish

Cucumber Cream

In a small strainer mix the cucumber and salt and let sit for 10 minutes over a bowl. In a mixer whip the cream until you have a stiff peak.

Squeeze the excess moisture from the cucumber. Fold the chives, vinegar, and pepper into the cream and refrigerate until the cakes are ready to serve.

Makes about ¾ cup.

⅓ cup cucumber, peeled, seeded, and finely diced

½ teaspoon kosher salt

½ cup heavy cream (see page 181)

2½ teaspoons minced chives

1 teaspoon white wine vinegar

Pinch white pepper

HECETA HEAD CRAB CAKES

Finally—the recipe you all have been waiting for! For decades people have been hounding us for this recipe and we have kept it a secret. It's not a complicated recipe and there really are no secret ingredients. There is just one ingredient that makes them so good, and that's lots of fresh Dungeness crab! We do not add anything that will overpower the subtle sweet taste of the crab. The rémoulade subtly complements as well, just a few garden herbs to enhance the flavors of our most treasured crustacean, the Dungeness.

Capered Rémoulade (recipe follows)

1 pound Oregon Dungeness crabmeat

¾ pound sole fillets

4 scallions

2 large eggs

6 tablespoons mayonnaise

Pinch hot paprika

4 shakes Tabasco

½ teaspoon ground mustard

1 cup fresh bread crumbs, divided
(see page 175)

1 tablespoon clarified butter
(see page 175)

If you buy the crabmeat already shelled, squeeze the meat slightly before using it to get rid of excess juices. Place the meat in a large mixing bowl, pick through it to remove any shells, and pull the meat apart, leaving a few chunks here and there. Cover and refrigerate until ready to use.

Steam the sole just until it starts to flake, but do not overcook. Refrigerate until completely cool.

Thinly slice the scallions just past the pale green portion and set aside.

Whisk the eggs in a mixing bowl. Add the mayonnaise, paprika, Tabasco, and mustard; mix thoroughly. Set aside.

When the sole is cool, flake it and mix it with the crabmeat. Add the scallions, egg mixture, and 2 tablespoons of the bread crumbs. Mix well but do not break down the crabmeat any further. You should be able to form a ball. If it seems a little loose, add more bread crumbs, not to exceed 4 tablespoons all together.

Put the remainder of the bread crumbs in a shallow pan or pie plate. Using a kitchen scale, take 2 ½ ounces of the crab mixture, form it into a ball, and place the ball in the bread crumbs. Cover the ball completely with crumbs; remove it from the pan. Shake off the excess, pat it into a cake, and place on a platter. Make 11 more cakes. Refrigerate until ready to serve.

Heat a 14-inch skillet to medium. Melt the butter; when it is hot, add the crab cakes. Cook each side until golden brown. Serve immediately with the rémoulade.

Makes 12 cakes.

Capered Rémoulade

In a small food processor place the garlic, parsley, chives, anchovy paste, and lemon juice and pulse. Add the mayonnaise and blend well, stopping to scrape down the sides. Add the capers and pulse a few times. Refrigerate for up to 1 week.

Makes about 1⅓ cups.

2 cloves garlic

1½ tablespoons chopped parsley

1½ tablespoons thinly snipped chives

½ teaspoon anchovy paste

3 teaspoons lemon juice

¾ cup mayonnaise

⅓ cup capers

Oregon Dungeness Crab, Fennel, Orange, and Avocado with Mango Curry Dressing

Oregon Dungeness crab really needs only one thing: crab crackers. The meat is so buttery and sweet that strong flavors can easily mask its delicate structure. We think this combination really plays well with the crab. We like grapeseed oil for this dish because it binds the dressing and holds the crab together without imparting a bold taste. It can be found in most specialty stores.

Dressing (recipe follows)

1 small fennel bulb

1 small orange, peeled and diced

1 avocado

6 ounces Dungeness crabmeat

1½ teaspoons grapeseed oil

Remove the outer layer from the fennel. Cut off the root end and stalks. Mince ½ teaspoon of the leafy part and save the rest for another use. Cut the bulb in half lengthwise and thinly slice the halves from the base up the stock.

Mix the orange, fennel, and minced leaf in a bowl and set aside.

Slice the avocado lengthwise into 18 pieces. Place 3 fanned slices on each plate. Make a bed of the fennel and orange mixture next to the slices.

Mix the crabmeat and oil and pile about 1 ounce onto the fennel bed. Dot the rim of the plate with about 1 tablespoon of the dressing and serve immediately.

Makes 6 servings.

Dressing

½ cup crème fraîche, (see page 176)

1 tablespoon plus 1 teaspoon mango chutney (see page 182)

2 cloves garlic

½ teaspoon Madras curry powder (see page 182)

¼ teaspoon turmeric

1 teaspoon rice wine vinegar

4 teaspoons water

3 teaspoons grapeseed oil

In a small food processor, combine the crème fraîche, chutney, garlic, curry powder, turmeric, vinegar, and water. Mix thoroughly, stopping to scrape the sides and bottom. With the processor on, add the oil to emulsify. Put in a small squeeze bottle and refrigerate until ready to use.

Makes about ¾ cup.

HERRING SALAD

We frequented a restaurant in Portland that served something close to this herring dish. Since we moved to the coast, we have still craved it, so we started making this recipe. Pickled herring is an acquired taste, and this dish is a good introduction to the delicacy. For this salad we use herring in white wine, not in sour cream.

Squeeze out the wine from the herring and onion. Put the herring and onion, apple, and sweet onion in a small food processor, reserving a few slivers of apple and sweet onion for garnish. Pulse to blend but do not make the mixture smooth. It should be slightly larger then relish.

Place the mixture in a decorative dish. Finely grate the egg over the salad, evenly distributing both white and yolk. Cut a sliver of apple and onion for garnish and place it in the center of the egg. Surround the dish with the radishes.

To serve, pass the herring with the bread and cream cheese.

Makes about 1 cup or 6 small servings.

½ cup herring and onions in wine

⅓ Fuji apple, peeled, cored, and cut into chunks

⅓ sweet onion, peeled and cut into chunks

1 hard-boiled egg

3 radishes, thinly sliced

Dark artisan rye bread, thinly sliced

Cream cheese

BAY SHRIMP BRUSCHETTA

2 cloves garlic, finely chopped

2 tablespoons finely chopped fresh basil

1 tablespoon finely chopped flat Italian parsley

1 tablespoon lemon juice

2 squirts Tabasco

¼ teaspoon salt

Several grinds fresh black pepper

¼ cup extra virgin olive oil, plus additional for brushing

3 medium-size tomatoes, peeled, seeded, and finely chopped

1 pound bay shrimp

1 loaf artisan sourdough or baguette

Diced kalamata olives

Fresh chives

When Oregon bay shrimp season is in full swing, so are the tomatoes. This bruschetta screams fresh!

In a large mixing bowl, combine the garlic, basil, parsley, lemon juice, Tabasco, salt, and pepper. Whisk in ¼ cup of the oil. Add the tomatoes and shrimp; mix thoroughly. Chill for several hours.

Thinly slice the bread to appetizer size, just big enough to hold a heaping tablespoon of the shrimp mixture. Brush the bread with the remaining oil and lightly grill or broil it. Mix the shrimp mixture again and measure out a heaping tablespoon. Lightly squeeze out any extra juice and mound the mixture on the bread. Top with the olives and a piece of chive. Serve immediately.

Makes about 16 bruschetta.

BAY SHRIMP MOUSSE

Oregon fisheries catch about 20 million pounds of bay shrimp a year, and according to the Marine Stewardship Council, our shrimp harvesting is certified as a sustainable practice. We can feel good about eating this mousse for two reasons: its creamy, rich taste and the fisheries' responsible fishing practices.

Place one-third of the scallions (the whitest part), cream cheese, chèvre, lemon juice, 4 sprigs of dill, a pinch of salt, and pepper in the bowl of a small food processor. Blend until creamy and smooth, stopping to scrape down the sides. Add ¾ cup of the shrimp and pulse; do not overblend. The mixture should be creamy but have some small bits of shrimp visible.

Transfer the mousse to a decorative bowl. Top with the remaining ¾ cup shrimp, the remaining scallions, and the remaining sprig of dill. Garnish with lemon slices. Serve on a plate with the cucumber and tomatoes. Pass around the table with the crumpets.

Makes 6 servings.

3 scallions, thinly sliced diagonally to the dark green part, divided

1½ ounces cream cheese

1 ounce plain chèvre

2 teaspoons lemon juice

5 small sprigs fresh dill, divided

Salt

Pinch white pepper

1½ cups bay shrimp, divided

Thinly sliced lemon, for garnish

Thinly sliced cucumbers

Grape or cherry tomatoes, halved lengthwise

6 warm crumpets

Scallop and Bay Shrimp Seviche

½ cup lime juice

½ cup lemon juice

2 pounds bay scallops

½ cup extra virgin olive oil

¼ cup thinly sliced scallions,
sliced to the dark green portion

2 cloves garlic, finely minced

1 shallot (about 1 tablespoon), minced

½ bunch fresh cilantro, chopped

¼ bunch fresh Italian parsley,
finely chopped

½ cup tomatillo sauce (see page 179)

1 teaspoon kosher salt

Freshly ground black pepper

1 pound bay shrimp

Avocado and tomato slices

As a side note: A friend once described this dish as thirst quenching. When Carol and Mike had the Strudel House, they would come to Newport for several days to research and write menus for the coming season. They always rented a condo with a kitchen so they could brainstorm and then cook up a storm. Michelle remembers these trips as one of her best childhood memories. This recipe was created on one of the trips, and it became a favorite birthday treat for Michelle. Now, living on the coast is like having those trips all the time, a favorite childhood memory every day.

Seviche is of Latin American origin and is prepared by cooking the seafood in citrus juice instead of heat. Most bay scallops are now farm raised and imported from Peru or Japan. When you buy them make sure they are "dry," meaning they have not been chemically treated to keep them moist. This treatment keeps the scallops from soaking up the citrus juices. Bay shrimp are cooked when they are processed. If soaked in citrus overnight, they will become tough. But when mixed with the cooked scallops, they will get just enough citrus to accent their buttery flavor.

Start making this dish the day before serving.

Pour the lime juice and lemon juice over the scallops and refrigerate overnight.

In a large bowl mix the oil, scallions, garlic, shallot, cilantro, parsley, tomatillo sauce, salt, and pepper to taste.

Drain the juice from the scallops and discard the juice. Add the scallops and shrimp to the dressing and mix well. Refrigerate for 2 hours. Serve in a decorative dish with the tomato and avocado slices.

Makes 8 to 10 servings.

House Smoked Albacore, Fresh Wasabi Mayonnaise, Watercress, and House Greens

We can't help but brag about Oregon, and this dish is all about those bragging rights. Albacore is one of the finest tunas, with its firm, rich meat. We alder smoke it just a bit, pan sear it to medium rare, chill it, and serve it thinly sliced.

Real wasabi has a taste worlds apart from imitation or powder forms, and it's processed fresh in Florence, Oregon! And watercress, both a wild and cultivated green in Oregon, is earthy and sweet. This combination, wrapped in greens from our garden, is bliss.

We use a salad spinner a lot at Heceta Head and recommend using one for all sorts of kitchen tasks. It really pulls the extra moisture off greens, herbs, and even potatoes and cut vegetables without damaging them. With greens we recommend washing, spinning, and then wrapping in a flour sack towel and refrigerating until ready to use.

8 butter lettuce cups, rinsed

4 ounces smoked albacore tuna, thinly sliced into 8 pieces

Wasabi Mayonnaise (recipe follows)

8 sprigs fresh watercress, rinsed

Place the lettuce cups on 8 individual plates Place a slice of tuna in each center. Add 1 teaspoon of mayonnaise and a sprig of watercress on top of each. Serve immediately.

Makes 8 small servings.

Wasabi Mayonnaise

2 large farm-fresh egg yolks

¾ teaspoon salt

½ teaspoon fresh wasabi paste

4 teaspoons ponzu or rice vinegar, divided

1½ cups vegetable oil, divided

4 teaspoons hot water, divided

In a small food processor thoroughly blend the egg yolks, salt, wasabi, and 3 teaspoons of the ponzu. Blend thoroughly. With the processor on, add the oil about ¼ cup at a time in a slow steady stream, checking to make sure it is emulsifying. It should appear smooth and creamy, not separated. Alternate with 1 teaspoon of the water after each ¼ cup of the oil. After ¾ cup of the oil has been added, stop to scrape down the sides and bottom. Turn the processor on and add the last teaspoon of vinegar. Continue alternating oil and water until they are all used.

Makes about 2 cups.

Oregon Lox Cheesecake
with Heirloom Tomato

When Michelle lived in Walla Walla, Washington, she had the privilege of cooking for a few winemakers' dinners. For a media tour dinner, she highlighted Oregon lox and Walla Walla sweet onion in this savory cheesecake. When she came to Heceta Head, she shared the recipe with her mom; it has become quite the hit at the breakfast table. When big, beautiful heirloom tomatoes and bright sweet peppers start showing up, the springform pan starts flying around the kitchen!

Preheat the oven to 350°F. Put 1 inch of hot water in a roasting pan large enough to place a 9-inch springform inside and place in the oven.

Prepare the springform pan: place parchment on the bottom; butter the sides and bottom. Wrap the bottom and up the sides of the pan with two large pieces of foil (to keep water from seeping in during the poaching process) and set aside.

Heat 2 tablespoons of the butter in a medium skillet over medium-low heat until hot. Add the onion and peppers and cook until soft, about 5 minutes. Set aside.

Mix the cream cheese and ricotta in a large mixing bowl. Add the eggs and scrape down the sides and bottom of the bowl. Add the cream and mix until combined. Fold in the lox, onion mixture, cheese, and salt. Pour into the prepared pan.

Place the pan in the roasting pan with the water; if needed add a little hot water to make the level about 1½ inches up the sides of the roasting pan. Bake for 1 hour and 15 minutes. Remove the cheesecake and then the roasting pan from the oven and turn off the heat. Remove the foil and return the cheesecake to the oven and let rest for 30 minutes. Remove from the oven and let cool on a wire rack. Refrigerate until firm; remove the springform and parchment. Serve well chilled in ½- to 1-inch wedges with the tomatoes.

Makes 12 to 24 servings.

Hot water

3 tablespoons unsalted butter, divided

1 cup diced sweet onion

¼ cup diced red pepper

¼ cup diced yellow pepper

¼ cup diced orange pepper

16 ounces cream cheese

15 ounces whole milk ricotta

5 large eggs

⅓ cup heavy cream (see page 181)

½ pound lox, chopped (see page 182)

¾ cup shredded Havarti cheese

¼ teaspoon kosher salt

Several slices heirloom tomato

Umpqua Oysters with Shallot and Brown Butter

Winchester Bay is home to some of the world's finest oyster beds, or should we say lines. Umpqua aquaculture suspends oysters on lines so they do not touch the ocean floor, which gives them a clean, creamy texture. For breakfast and as an appetizer for weddings, we serve these little treasures with browned butter and shallots. We also like to barbecue oysters in the shell and drizzle them with the butter-shallot combination.

In a small saucepan, heat the butter and allow it to bubble until it starts to turn brown, 7 to 10 minutes. Remove from the heat and let cool slightly. Pass the butter through a fine- mesh sieve or cheesecloth to remove the browned milk solids. Return the butter to the saucepan and heat on medium low. Add the shallot and cook slowly until it is soft; do not caramelize. Set aside.

Preheat the oven to 350°F. Place the oysters in a Pyrex dish or casserole and pour the wine over them. Bake for 5 to 7 minutes, just to lightly poach them.

Place each oyster on a serving dish (we use the oyster shell or a flat bottom Chinese soup spoon) and spoon the butter and shallots over the top. Serve immediately.

Serves 10 to 12 people.

½ cup unsalted butter

2 tablespoons finely chopped shallot

24 extra-small oysters

1 cup dry white wine

Freshly ground sea salt

UMPQUA OYSTERS GRATIN

If you love oysters, this is a really comforting way to eat them. If you are not an oyster fan, this recipe may just change your mind.

2 cups spinach

2 strips alder-smoked pepper bacon

1 clove garlic, finely minced

⅓ cup dry white wine

⅓ cup heavy cream (see page 181)

16 extra-small oysters, with nectar

4 teaspoons Parmigiano Reggiano cheese

Salt and pepper

12 teaspoons fresh bread crumbs, divided (see page 175)

4 teaspoons unsalted butter, melted

Freshly chopped Italian parsley

Sourdough bread, toasted

Wash the spinach and tap dry, leaving a little water on the leaves. In a large skillet over medium-low heat cook the spinach until wilted; with the cover on, set aside to cool. Squeeze the spinach to release excess liquid.

Dice the bacon and cook until crisp. Drain, reserving the fat.

Preheat the oven to 400°F. In a medium saucepan, heat the reserved bacon fat and add the garlic and spinach. Sauté until the garlic is soft. Add the wine and simmer until reduced by half. Add the cream and oyster nectar and simmer on low for about 5 to 7 minutes. Add the cheese, salt, and pepper to taste.

Mix the bread crumbs and butter in a small bowl.

Place 2 oysters in eight 4-ounce ramekins and divide the spinach mixture and diced bacon among them. Place 1½ teaspoons of the bread crumbs on top of each. Place all ramekins on a baking sheet and bake for 10 minutes. Sprinkle a bit of parsley on each and serve with the bread.

Makes 8 servings.

FRAPPÉS

FRAPPÉS ARE SERVED TO CLEANSE PALATES
after the seafood course and prepare guests for the main dish. Each serving is small, because some frappés are as rich as a sorbet. Yogurt is present to make the drink smooth, and just a bit of honey or sugar enhances the fruit flavor.

While on the island of Penang in Malaysia, Steven and Michelle had the most amazing watermelon shakes and brought the idea home. Michelle has integrated frozen watermelon into many recipes, so we get a refreshing melon texture and subtle sweetness instead of using ice or water. We have also found that using frozen fruits for all of the frappés keeps the drinks colder. Even when fruit is available fresh, we prefer to freeze it before we make the drink.

We love our berries and melons all year-round; unfortunately, they have a shorter season then we prefer. So when berries are available by the flat, we wash them, let them dry, and spread them onto a sheet pan in a single layer and freeze them in the deep freeze. Just after they freeze we put then in freezer storage containers. Blueberries freeze the best and raspberries are the most fragile, but they are both wonderful in December! (See page 177 for freezing berries.)

BLUEBERRY CITRUS WHITE CHOCOLATE

This is our most popular frappé. Frozen blueberries also make a great snack, kind of like hard candy but with lots of goodness for your body and brain. This recipe calls for half a lemon zested and juiced. It is much easier to zest a lemon whole before juicing. See page 184 for zest.

1 cup whole milk yogurt

½ lemon zest and juice

3 tablespoons white chocolate syrup, such as Monin (see page 183)

2 cups frozen blueberries, divided

1 cup frozen watermelon

1 to 1½ cups apple or white grape juice, divided

Freshly whipped heavy cream (see page 181)

Put the yogurt, lemon juice, syrup, blueberries (reserving 6 for garnish), watermelon, and ⅓ of the apple or grape juice in a blender. Blend and gradually add just enough juice to make the mixture smooth. Serve in pretty, clear glasses topped with the cream and garnished with lemon zest and a blueberry.

Makes 6 small servings.

PEACH ROSE LASSI

Lassis are of Indian origin and are traditionally served to soothe the palate while eating extremely hot curry. When Michelle and Steven were in South-east Asia, they tried several types of lassi. The most popular was mango, but tomato and cucumber were also quite prevalent. Try this recipe with your favorite fruits and flavors such as honey, rose water, or orange blossom water. Our favorite is made with fresh local peaches when they are almost overripe with sweetness. When they're blended with the yogurt and rose water, the only way to describe the outcome is "supernatural!"

2½ cups whole milk yogurt

2 cups fresh peaches

½ cup sugar

⅛ teaspoon rose water (see page 183)

30 (about 2½ cups) ice cubes

Freshly whipped heavy cream (see page 181)

Rose petals, for garnish

Place the yogurt, peaches, sugar, and rose water in a blender and blend well. Add the ice and blend until smooth. If the lassi seems a little thick, add water a little at a time until the consistency is to your liking. Serve in pretty, clear glasses topped with the cream and garnished with a sliver of peach and rose petal.

Makes 6 small servings.

CAPE BLANCO CRANBERRY PASSION FRUIT

The berries from the Cape Blanco Cranberry Company are vine ripened, deep red, sweet, and tart but not the slightest bit bitter.

In Newport there is a great Asian market where we found passion fruit syrup. Mai's Asian Market has products from all over the world, and Mai has a lot of good advice to give as well. Passion fruit syrup can be found in Asian food stores or frozen as a puree in specialty food stores.

In a blender thoroughly mix the syrup, yogurt, and 1 cup of the apple juice. Add the cranberries (reserving 3 for garnish) and watermelon and blend again, adding just enough apple juice to make it smooth but not too much or it will separate.

Serve in pretty, clear glasses topped with the cream and garnished with the apricot and a cranberry half.

Makes 6 small servings.

½ cup passion fruit syrup
(see page 183)

½ cup whole milk yogurt

1 to 1½ cups apple juice, divided

½ cup frozen cranberries, divided

1½ cups frozen watermelon

Freshly whipped cream

Slivered dried apricots

STRAWBERRY CANDIED GINGER AND FRESH MINT

Fresh mint grows like a weed, and it's a weed we'll always invite. Steven has about 20 varieties; all are nice to play with in different foods and drinks.

The best way to tell whether you want to use a particular herb for a dish is to take a bit from the plant, bruise it between your fingers, close your eyes, and smell the fragrance while thinking about the foods you want to use it with. Does it still sound like a good match? Then try it out.

3 small chunks candied ginger, divided (see page 181)

1 to 1½ cups water, divided

¾ cup whole milk yogurt

⅓ cup sugar

3 cups frozen strawberries

6 fresh mint leaves, coarsely chopped

Freshly whipped cream

6 mint buds

In a blender mix the ginger (reserving 6 slivers for garnish), 1 cup of the water, yogurt, and sugar until well blended. Add the strawberries and just enough additional water to make a smooth consistency. Add the mint leaves and blend just until mixed.

Serve in pretty, clear glasses topped with the cream and garnished with a sliver of the candied ginger and the mint bud.

Makes 6 small servings.

HIBISCUS, MELON, AND WILDFLOWER HONEY

When Michelle had a coffee shop in Walla Walla, Washington, she made hibiscus cooler during the summer. We froze the cooler into cubes and added them to this frappé. Hibiscus tastes a bit tart and earthy; mixed with melon and local honey, it's very refreshing. This cooler is also good with fresh mint and served with rum or used to make sangria.

Prepare the hibiscus cubes the day before serving the frappé.

Mix the honey and water. When they are completely incorporated, blend in a blender. Add the yogurt, hibiscus cubes, melon (reserving some for garnish), and about ½ cup of water. Blend and add more water as needed for a smooth consistency.

Serve in pretty, clear glasses topped with the cream and garnished with a small piece of melon, and a hibiscus tea leaf.

Makes 6 small servings.

Hibiscus Tea Cooler

In an 8-cup measuring cup, pour the water over the flowers and sugar and steep for 1 hour. Strain the tea into ice cube trays and freeze. Store the cubes in freezer bags up to 6 months.

Makes 3 standard ice cube trays.

3 Hibiscus Tea Cooler cubes (recipe follows)

2 tablespoons wildflower honey (see page 182)

2 tablespoons warm water

¾ cup whole milk yogurt

3 cups frozen Galia or other pale melon, divided

Whipped cream

Hibiscus leaf

4 cups boiling water

1 cup dried hibiscus tea flowers

1 cup sugar

Avocado Lime

1 avocado, peeled and pitted

2 tablespoons lime juice

⅓ cup whole milk yogurt

⅓ cup sweetened condensed milk

40 (about 3 cups) ice cubes

Whipped cream

6 small lime slivers, for garnish

This is a rich and comforting concoction that should be served very cold. The buttery avocado and the tart lime are welcoming palate cleansers.

Put the avocado, juice, yogurt, condensed milk, and ice cubes in a blender and blend until very smooth.

Serve immediately in pretty, clear glasses topped with the cream and garnished with a lime sliver.

Makes 6 small servings.

Dagoba Chocolate and Raspberry

This Ashland, Oregon, company has some of the most original chocolate flavors we've ever tasted. The company's syrup also contains all organic ingredients and is a fair trade product. (see page 185). Paired with fresh raspberry juice, this frappé is like a truffle in a glass. When raspberries are in season, we try to make as much juice as possible, a race to preserve the raspberry flavor for the entire year.

Blend the juice, yogurt, and syrup (reserving a bit for drizzling) in a blender. Add the watermelon, and with the blender running add the water until the mixture is smooth.

Serve in pretty, clear glasses topped with the cream and garnished with a raspberry, and a drizzle of chocolate syrup.

Makes 6 small servings.

⅓ cup Raspberry Juice (recipe follows)

½ cup whole milk yogurt

⅓ cup chocolate syrup, divided

1½ cups frozen watermelon

⅓ cup water

Whipped cream

Raspberries, for garnish

Raspberry Juice

In a medium pot, simmer the berries over medium-low heat until they are completely soft and soupy. Remove from the heat and set aside to cool.

Using a mill, china cap, or fine-mesh strainer, seed the raspberries. When you have a seedy mass that looks like jam, add about one-third of the water, pressing the seeds against the strainer and using the water to help release any extra juice. Add more water and repeat. When finished the seeds should look pretty barren of any juice or fruit. Discard the seeds.

Refrigerate for up to 1 week, or freeze in ice cubes trays and store in freezer bags for up to 3 months.

Makes about 3 cups or 2 standard ice cube trays.

3 cups raspberries

1 cup water, divided

PEAR WITH ORANGE BLOSSOM HONEY
AND CARDAMOM

Glory Bee Honey in Eugene, Oregon, has 28 varieties of honey, all with unique tastes and sweetness but always 100 percent pure. The company also sells beekeeping equipment and books, candle-making supplies, and organic bulk foods.

Pear puree is nice to have for drinks, desserts, and sauces. Depending on the pears you use and how ripe they are, you will need to adjust the sugar. For this reason we add the sugar after we pureed the pears but while the puree is still warm so the sugar will melt and we can taste for sweetness.

Prepare the pear puree at least a day before serving the frappé.

¼ cup warm water

2 tablespoons orange blossom honey (see page 182)

¼ teaspoon ground cardamom, plus additional for garnish

8 cubes Pear Puree (recipe follows)

⅓ cup whole milk yogurt

8 ice cubes or ½ cup water

Whipped cream

Fresh pear slivers for garnish

Mix the water, honey, and cardamom. Place the mixture in a blender with the pear puree cubes, yogurt, and ice cubes; blend until smooth. Add water if the drink is too thick.

Serve in pretty, clear glasses topped with the cream and garnished with pear slivers, and a dash of cardamom.

Makes 6 small servings.

Pear Puree

15 pounds Bartlett, Seckel, or other sweet pear

1½ cups water

2 cups sugar, divided

Quarter, core, and peel the pears. Put them in a large pot, cover with the water, and bring to a boil. Reduce the heat to simmer and cook until the pears are very tender, about 20 minutes. Strain off the liquid and pass the pears through a mill while they are still warm. Add 1 cup of the sugar, stir for a minute to melt the sugar, and taste the puree. Continue adding sugar and tasting for desired sweetness.

Freeze in ice cube trays and store in freezer containers for up to 2 months.

Makes about 8 cups or 6 standard ice cube trays.

EGGS

THE MAIN COURSE, the perfect morning fare, eggs. Farm fresh eggs make a huge difference in all our dishes. They have deep yellow, rich yolks and taste as though they already have been buttered and salted.

These dishes are all vegetarian so we can highlight meat separately. We also use as many local cheeses and fresh herbs and produce as pos-sible, keeping the dishes simple so each ingredient pops and has a moment to shine.

We included three frittata recipes in this chapter. We have seen many methods for making frittatas, and although this version may be a bit American, it is our favorite. The trick is not to cook the eggs too quickly. If you cook them slowly and gently fold them, you will end up with lots of creamy layers. Remember to remove the frit-tata from the heat just a little before the eggs are cooked through because they will continue cooking for a bit.

SPINACH, KALE, AND JUNIPER GROVE FETA FRITTATA

Juniper Grove Cheese has mastered the art of making feta. It is a creamy, full-flavored, and perfectly salted cheese. And because it is a salty cheese, no salt is added to the eggs. Steven grows beautiful bunches of rich Japanese kale and spinach in our kitchen garden. We mix them with farm fresh eggs to make one of our signature dishes.

12 large eggs

3 tablespoons mayonnaise

1 tablespoon clarified butter (see page 175)

2 teaspoons finely chopped shallot

3 medium kale greens, ribs removed and coarsely chopped

⅓ cup baby spinach

¼ cup crumbled feta

¼ cup crème fraîche (see page 176)

3 sun-dried tomatoes, julienned

In a large bowl whisk the eggs with the mayonnaise until airy. Set aside.

Preheat the broiler to high. Heat a 10-inch nonstick skillet over medium heat. Add the butter and shallot; cook until the shallot sweats. Add the kale and cook over medium-low heat until wilted and soft, about 5 minutes. Increase the heat to medium and add the eggs. Let them set a bit, but do not let them brown. (If they are getting brown, the temperature is too high.) With a rubber spatula, push the eggs from the bottom and sides and let the next layer of egg go to the bottom and set. Repeat until all the eggs are soft. Take the skillet off the heat.

Pile the spinach in the middle of the skillet and fold the eggs over the top to cover. Let the spinach steam in the eggs for about 2 minutes. Fold the spinach into the eggs, equally dispersing the spinach, but do not mix too much. Return the skillet to the heat for about 1 to 2 minutes to set the eggs. The frittata should easily come away from the pan. Sprinkle the feta over the top.

Place the skillet under the broiler with the handle sticking out of the oven. Broil until the feta starts to brown and the eggs are set. Run a rubber spatula around the skillet rim to loosen the sides, tilt the skillet, and slide the frittata onto a serving platter. Cut into 6 pieces and garnish each with the crème fraîche and tomato. Using a pie server, serve one piece to each guest.

Makes 6 servings.

POTATO, SWISS CHARD, AND ROSEMARY FRITTATA

Every summer we look forward to visiting Johnson's Farm in Eugene, Oregon. Starting in June it seems with every visit there is a new berry or fresh produce to pick from, including a huge barrel of new potatoes. Michelle paws through the potatoes looking for the smallest reds and whites because she knows they will be the sweetest and creamiest of the bunch. Back at Heceta Head we roast the potatoes in olive oil for 30 to 40 minutes, roll them in freshly chopped rosemary and parsley, and sprinkle them with kosher salt. Hot out of the oven, the skins just burst and release the most creamy potato goodness. The next day they are just as wonderful because the herbs have infused the potato. Steven's garden bursts with large bunches of rainbow colored chard. Our farm fresh eggs are a perfect vehicle for this combination.

Prepare the potatoes and set aside.

In a large bowl whisk the eggs with the mayonnaise until airy. Set aside. Preheat the broiler to high.

Heat a 10-inch nonstick skillet over medium heat. Add the butter and onion and cook until the onion is soft. Add the potatoes, reserving 6 slices for garnish, and cook over medium heat until light brown, about 5 to 7 minutes. Add the chard and sauté until it is wilted and soft. Add the eggs and let them set a bit, but do not let them brown. (If they are getting brown, the temperature is too high.) With a rubber spatula, push the eggs from the bottom and sides and let the next layer go to the bottom and set. Repeat until all the eggs are soft. Let them sit about 1 to 2 minutes to set the eggs. The frittata should easily come away from the pan. Sprinkle the Pecorino Romano over the top.

Place the skillet under the broiler with the handle sticking out of the oven. Broil until the Pecorino Romano starts to brown and the eggs are set. Run a rubber spatula around the skillet rim to loosen the sides, tilt the skillet, and slide the frittata onto a serving platter. Cut into 6 pieces. Garnish with a dollop of crème fraîche, a thin slice of potato, and a sprig of rosemary. Using a pie server, serve a piece to each guest.

Makes 6 servings.

3 baby red potatoes,
roasted with rosemary and Italian parsley, thinly sliced, divided

12 large eggs

3 tablespoons mayonnaise

1 tablespoon clarified butter
(see page 175)

⅓ sweet onion, diced

2 leaves Swiss chard leaves,
ribs removed, washed and chopped

¼ cup finely grated Pecorino Romano

¼ cup crème fraîche (see page 176)

6 fresh rosemary sprigs, for garnish

SHIRRED EGGS WITH OREGON WHITE TRUFFLES

Truffles are like the platinum of the mushroom world: rare, luxurious, and expensive. For centuries in Europe this earthy and seductive fungus has been celebrated as one of its most precious and gourmet foods. The Oregon truffle is gaining in popularity and esteem and is almost parallel to French and Italian truffles, yet lucky for us at a fifth the price! The truffles take this simple dish of eggs, ricotta, yellow squash, and cream and turns it into a sensuous and heady morning affair.

There are a couple of ways to achieve the truffle flavor for this dish. When fresh truffles come to us they are still covered in dirt and are flavorless. As they mature they become more and more fragrant—so fragrant that they have the ability to permeate most of the contents of the refrigerator, so take heed! After we scrub and wash the little nubbins, we keep them fresh (tightly sealed in a glass jar) and finely grate them for a garnish just before serving. Because of their aromatic structure, heating them would take away the flavor. As the truffles mature, we keep some in a container with eggs or cheese or even rice; the truffle flavor will pass through the food and flavor it. When the truffles have reached full maturity, they must be used before they spoil so we freeze them in butter. If truffles are allowed to ripen past their full bloom, they take on an acrid ammonia-like intensity. Taste your butter before adding it to a dish for it can be very strong. Just a touch of truffle butter will flavor individual servings.

~

2 tablespoons shallot, finely minced

4 teaspoons butter, divided

1 yellow squash or zucchini

½ cup whole milk ricotta cheese

3 tablespoons shredded Gouda or fontina cheese

1 tablespoon finely grated Pecorino Romano cheese

Freshly ground black pepper

Pinch salt

6 large eggs, at room temperature

6 teaspoons cream

Boiling water

1 fresh truffle or six drops of truffle butter

12 small toast points

Preheat the oven to 350°F and butter six 6-ounce ramekins. In a small skillet over low heat, cook the shallot in 2 teaspoons of the butter until soft. Set aside.

With a mandoline or Japanese peeler, slice the squash lengthwise no more than ⅛ inch thick. Set aside.

In a medium mixing bowl, combine three cheeses, pepper, salt, and shallot.

Line the sides of the ramekins with a layer of the squash. Divide the ricotta mixture among the ramekins, about 2 tablespoons per serving. Make a well in the center of the ricotta so it lies against the squash. Crack 1 egg into the middle of each ramekin and cover with 1 teaspoon of the cream. Sprinkle with a little salt and place the ramekins in a 9-by-13-inch baking pan. Add the boiling water until it is halfway up the sides of the ramekins. Bake for 20 minutes.

Place a couple of fresh truffle shavings or a drop of truffle butter on each ramekin. Serve with the toast points.

Makes 6 servings.

EGGS VOL-AU-VENT

Meaning "windblown," this is a perfect dish to serve on the Oregon Coast. As delicate as vol-au-vents are, it would not take much for these baskets to take flight. Delicate asparagus acts as "anchors" for soft scramble farm fresh eggs and Willamette Valley Cheese Havarti.

When we have truffles in season, the asparagus is really wonderful with truffle shavings or drizzled in a little truffle butter or oil.

Vol-au-vents (recipe follows)

8 large eggs

¼ cup heavy cream (see page 181)

12 asparagus tips

Ice cubes

1 tablespoon plus 2 teaspoons clarified butter, divided (see page 175)

1 shallot, thinly sliced

⅓ cup Havarti, shredded

Kosher salt

Freshly ground pepper

⅛ teaspoon truffle shavings, butter, or oil (optional, if available)

Take the vol-au-vents from the oven and with a very sharp serrated knife (a grapefruit knife works well), cut the middle out of the vol-au-vents, leaving the decorative borders and bottoms. Place them in a warm oven until ready to serve.

In a large mixing bowl whisk the eggs until airy. Add the cream and whisk again. Set aside.

In a skillet bring 2 inches of water to a boil. Cut the woody ends from the asparagus, usually about an inch from the bottom. With a vegetable peeler, peel the asparagus stems to a point, like sharpening a pencil. When the water is boiling, add the asparagus and cook until just al dente, from 30 seconds to 2 minutes depending on the size of the asparagus. They should be bright green and just slightly cooked. Drain in a colander with a couple of ice cubes and run cold water over them to stop the cooking. Set aside.

In a medium sauté pan, melt 1 tablespoon of the butter; add the shallot and cook until soft. Set aside.

Heat the remaining 2 teaspoons of butter in a large nonstick skillet over medium heat. Whisk the eggs again to add a little more air; add to the skillet. Slowly cook the eggs, moving them with a rubber spatula so they stay creamy and do not overcook. When they are still very soft but starting to set, fold the cheese into the eggs. Remove from the burner; the eggs will continue to cook and this dish is meant to have very soft scrambled eggs. Set aside.

Return the shallots to medium-high heat; when hot add the asparagus. Sauté for a few minutes just to get them hot. Season to taste with salt and pepper. Turn off the heat and add the truffle shavings.

Place 1 vol-au-vent on each plate. Gently spoon the eggs into them. Top with 3 pieces of asparagus and some shallot. Serve immediately.

Makes 4 servings.

Vol-au-vents

Preheat the oven to 400°F and oil a baking sheet with baking spray. Set aside.

With a sharp knife, cut a ⅓-inch border inside the edge of the pastry, leaving 2 opposite corners intact. Starting with a cut corner, fold the border over and align it with the inside edge of the opposite side. Do the same with the opposite cut border to overlap the dough and align it on the edge of the opposite side. (See accompanying photograph.) Pick up the pastry square, and with a pastry brush lightly brush with the egg wash. Place it on the baking sheet. Repeat with the other squares.

Bake for 10 minutes. Reduce the heat to 375°F and bake for another 8 minutes. Turn off the oven, but keep them in the oven until the eggs are prepared.

Makes 4 vol-au-vent shells.

Four 5-by-5-inch squares all-butter puff pastry

1 large egg whisked with

¼ teaspoon water

EGGS BANDITO

This recipe was created in part by our crazy Aunt Irene. She was so frugal that even stale corn chips were put to use. She made this dish for herself and her dog, Missy (named after her great-niece, guess who?). It's a fun dish with the crunch, and it's a crowd pleaser. We've added lots of fresh ingredients and we like the chips fresh. Aunt Irene used to make a heaping scramble. We've adapted it to fit our frittata recipe.

12 large eggs

1 teaspoon lime juice

1 cup corn chips, slightly crushed

¼ teaspoon ground cumin

1 cup Pepper Jack

½ cup salsa verde or tomatillo sauce
(see page 179)

1 tablespoon chopped fresh cilantro

¼ cup seeded and diced fresh tomato

¼ cup sour cream

6 slices avocado

Turn on the broiler and set the rack in the highest position. In a large bowl whisk the eggs with the lime juice until they are light and airy. Set aside.

Toast the corn chips and cumin in a 10-inch nonstick skillet over medium heat. When they are slightly browned, add the eggs. With a rubber spatula, push the eggs from the bottom and off the sides to form layers. Cook them slowly; when they are still soft but are holding shape, let them sit on the burner for 1 to 2 minutes to set the bottom. The frittata should easily come away from the pan. Remove from the heat. Spread the salsa evenly across the top but do not mix into the eggs. Sprinkle the cheese over the salsa. Place the skillet under the broiler for 1 to 2 minutes to melt the cheese, keeping the oven door open and the skillet handle sticking out.

Run a rubber spatula around the skillet rim to loosen the sides, tilt the skillet, and slide the frittata onto a serving platter. Cut into 6 pieces and sprinkle the cilantro and tomato over the top. Place 1 tablespoon of the sour cream on each slice and 1 avocado slice propped on the sour cream. Using a pie server, serve a piece to each guest.

Makes 6 servings.

EGGS BENEDICT

There are endless possibilities for eggs Benedict. We have veered from the traditional Canadian bacon and English muffin because there are so many interesting breads and toppings to use. In Oregon we are blessed with an abundance of wild chanterelle mushrooms and several amazing wineries. The following combination highlights both as well as our garden herbs. With the seven-course breakfast we serve one egg per person. If you are serving this without the other courses, we recommend two eggs per person.

Keep the hollandaise sauce warm in the top of a double boiler on very low heat; check the temperature often so the sauce does not cook further. Keep the mushrooms covered with foil in the oven on warm, about 175°F.

Slice the bread into eight 4-by-3-inch pieces. Put the bread on a baking sheet and set aside.

Remove the mushrooms from the oven, but keep them covered with the foil. Turn the broiler to high.

In a wide but fairly shallow pot bring about 4 inches of water and the vinegar to a boil. Poach the eggs (see page 176) and put them in a dish just big enough to hold them all. While the eggs are poaching, lightly toast the bread on both sides under the boiler. Line up 4 plates and place 2 toasts on each plate. With a slotted spoon gently shake off any excess water from a poached egg and place it on the toast. Repeat for all the eggs.

Cover each egg with a spoonful of hollandaise sauce. Spoon the mushroom mixture over the sauce. Garnish with a thyme sprig and serve immediately.

Makes 4 servings.

1 cup Hollandaise Sauce
(recipe follows)

Chanterelle Mushroom Sauté (recipe follows)

1 small loaf artisan sourdough or other rustic bread

3 tablespoons vinegar

8 eggs, at room temperature

4 fresh thyme sprigs

Hollandaise (or Mousseline) Sauce

This classic recipe of eggs and butter can be intimidating to the home cook. Emulsifying the butter without scrambling the eggs tends to scare people. But fret not! At Heceta Head we use two methods: traditional (over a double boiler) and in a blender.

When we add heavy cream to hollandaise, it becomes mousseline sauce, which we prefer to serve. Here we use the blender method, hoping it will help ease anxiety.

In a saucepan that will pour easily, bring the butter to a bubble but do not brown.

Put the egg yolks, lemon, pepper, salt, and Tabasco in a blender. Blend thoroughly. When the butter is bubbling vigorously, with the blender running add about one-quarter of the butter in a slow steady stream. Let it blend for about 5 seconds to make sure the emulsion is happening. With the blender running, slowly pour in the remaining butter. As soon as the butter is incorporated, turn off the blender. Now you have hollandaise sauce. If you want mousseline sauce, turn on the blender and quickly add the cream. As soon as it is mixed in, turn off the blender.

To hold the sauce, put it in the top of a double boiler over warm water. Just before serving heat the water to a simmer and whisk the sauce until it is smooth and warm enough to spoon over the eggs.

Makes 1 cup.

5 tablespoons unsalted butter

3 large egg yolks

1 tablespoon lemon juice

Dash white pepper

¼ teaspoon kosher salt

2 squirts Tabasco

¼ cup heavy cream (see page 181)

Chanterelle Mushroom Sauté

Remove dirt and pine needles from the mushrooms with a brush. (Use water only if absolutely necessary, for water can make them soggy.) If the buttons are small, halve or quarter them. If they are larger, slice them ¼ inch thick, nickel to quarter size.

Melt the butter in a sauté pan over medium heat. Add the shallot and sauté until it sweats. Meanwhile, bruise the thyme between your fingers over the pan and let it fall over the shallot. Add the mushrooms and sauté over medium-high heat for about 10 minutes, until the mushrooms have lost most of their moisture. Add the wine and sauté a few more minutes until the wine has evaporated. Add the salt and pepper to taste.

Transfer to a plate and keep warm until the eggs are done.

Makes about 1 cup.

½ pound fresh chanterelle mushrooms, cleaned

2 tablespoons clarified butter (see page 175)

1 large shallot, thinly sliced in rounds

¼ teaspoon thyme

2 tablespoons Chardonnay or other dry white wine

Kosher salt

Freshly ground pepper

Bread Toppings

If chanterelle mushrooms are not in season we have a variety of other bread toppings to choose. These are just a few of our favorite Benedict bread toppings. To include them all would require a book of its own! These toppings don't stop at Benedicts, though. Spread on a hunk of hearty bread and with a glass of wine, they are a nice start to any meal.

KALAMATA OLIVE AND ROASTED RED PEPPER TAPENADE

4 sprigs Italian parsley

2 cloves garlic

2 tablespoons extra virgin olive oil

¾ cup kalamata olives, pitted

2 roasted red peppers, seeded and roughly cut into 2-inch pieces (see page 178)

Freshly ground black pepper

In a small food processor, combine the parsley, garlic, and oil; pulse. Stop to push down the ingredients from the sides with a spatula. Add the olives and pulse several times. Add the peppers and 4 or 5 grinds of pepper. Pulse just until the mixture is spreadable but not a paste. Spread this topping on the bread after it is broiled and lay the poached egg so some of the topping is showing.

Makes about 1 cup.

ARUGULA AND ROASTED OREGON HAZELNUT PESTO

1 pound arugula, washed and stemmed

3 cloves garlic

2 tablespoons lemon juice

½ cup finely grated Pecorino

2 tablespoons roasted hazelnuts, roughly chopped (see page 178)

¼ teaspoon kosher salt

Freshly ground black pepper

½ cup extra virgin olive oil

While the arugula is still a little damp from washing, place it in a skillet, cover, and cook over medium-low heat for a few minutes to let it sweat. With tongs turn it so it cooks evenly. Cook until it is completely wilted and soft but still bright green. Transfer to a strainer; when it is cool, squeeze the arugula to release the extra juices. Set aside.

In a small food processor, pulse the garlic and lemon juice a few times. Add the arugula, Pecorino, hazelnuts, salt, and pepper; pulse to blend. When it is roughly blended, add the oil. Adjust the salt and pepper to taste. Spread this topping on the bread after it is broiled and lay the poached egg so some of the topping is showing.

Makes about 1½ cups.

ARTICHOKE HEART ANTIPASTO

Drain the artichoke hearts, squeeze out all extra moisture, and put them in a medium bowl. They may have leaves attached; if they are not tough, keep them intact. Chop the hearts into ½-inch pieces and add the lemon juice.

Stack the basil leaves in one direction. Starting at the stem side, roll them up. As thinly as you can, slice across the rolled leaves, making very thin ribbons or a chiffonade. Add to the artichokes with the oil, parsley, garlic, capers, and cheese; mix to create a chunky spread. Add the salt and pepper to taste. Spread this topping on the bread after it is broiled and lay the poached egg so some of the topping is showing.

Makes about 1¾ cups.

1 cup artichoke hearts, packed in water

2 teaspoons lemon juice

8 medium fresh basil leaves

⅓ cup extra virgin olive oil

2 sprigs fresh Italian parsley, finely chopped

1 small clove garlic, minced

2 teaspoons capers, roughly chopped

⅓ cup finely grated Parmigiano Reggiano

¼ teaspoon kosher salt

Freshly ground black pepper

EGGS HECETA

We call this dish Eggs Heceta because historically it was possible to procure every ingredient from the lightstation grounds. Cows were raised for milk, cream, and cheese. Chickens were raised for eggs. A ship brought light keepers their stipends, which included grains for baking bread. And now we have Steven's beautiful garden that produces rosemary and the richest broccoli. Where would we procure the wakame seaweed? From our front-yard garden, the Pacific Ocean.

This strata is made the day before it is served so the eggs and cream can soak the bread, which gives the dish a rich and custardlike consistency. Strata can be made in a 9-by-9-inch casserole or individual serving dishes. For our seven-course breakfast, we prefer individual servings for the presentation.

4 large eggs

1 cup whole milk

½ cup heavy cream (see page 181)

1 teaspoon finely chopped fresh rosemary

1½ teaspoons finely chopped dried wakame (see page 183)

¼ teaspoon kosher salt

5 ounces (about 2 cups cubed) ciabatta or other hearty bread

3 ounces (about 1 cup) shredded medium cheddar

3 ounces (about 1 cup) shredded Gruyère

1 cup bite-size broccoli florets

2 teaspoons chopped fresh Italian parsley

In a large mixing bowl whisk the eggs until light. Add the milk and cream and whisk thoroughly. Add the rosemary, wakame, and salt. Set aside.

Cut the bread into ½-inch cubes (to make about 2 cups) and put half into a 9-by-9-inch dish. Layer the cheddar, Gruyère, and broccoli over the bread. Pour the egg mixture over the top and add the remaining bread cubes, pressing them so they can soak up the eggs. Cover and refrigerate overnight.

Preheat the oven to 350°F and oil six 8-ounce ramekins with baking spray. Divide the strata among the ramekins, place them on a baking sheet, and bake for 20 minutes. Turn the baking sheet and bake for another 20 minutes. The strata is done when the tops are golden brown and have risen very high. Turn out and place right side up onto individual plates. Garnish with the parsley.

Makes 6 servings.

Sweet Potato, Sage, and Juniper Grove Smoked Chèvre Strata

This baked egg dish is made the day before it is served so the eggs and cream can soak into the bread, which gives the dish a rich and custardlike consistency. Strata can be made in a casserole or in individual servings. For our seven-course breakfast, we prefer individual servings for the presentation.

Cheese-maker Pierre Kolisch makes some of the finest goat cheese in Oregon. One of our favorites is his Thor's Special Smoked Crottin (see page 185). It is nutty, sharp, creamy, and smoky. This dish is rich with butter and sage and slightly sweet with the sweet potato and caramelized onion. When you get the little smoked chèvre surprise in the middle, the combination is magic.

½ medium sweet onion

3 tablespoons unsalted butter

4 leaves fresh sage, roughly chopped

5 ounces (about 2 cups cubed) ciabatta or other hearty bread

4 large eggs

1 cup whole milk

½ cup heavy cream (see page 181)

¼ teaspoon salt

1½ cups sweet potato cut into ½-inch cubes

5 ounces (about 1½ cups) shredded extra sharp cheddar

2 ounces (about ¼ cup) smoked chèvre

6 fresh sage sprigs

Slice the onion and sauté in the butter. When the onion is almost caramelized add the sage. Cook until the onion is caramelized.

Cut the bread into 1-inch cubes (to make about 2 cups) and toss with the onion mixture until coated. Set aside.

In a large mixing bowl, whisk the eggs until light and airy. Add the milk, cream, and salt. Whisk again.

Place half the bread mixture on the bottom of a 9-by-9-inch dish. Layer the sweet potato then the cheddar cheese evenly over the bread. Pour the egg mixture over the top; add the remaining bread mixture. Press on the bread a bit so it can soak up the eggs. Cover and refrigerate overnight.

Preheat the oven to 350°F and oil six 8-ounce ramekins with baking spray. Divide the strata among the ramekins, making sure to get all layers into each ramekin. Push ½ ounce chèvre into the center of each strata.

Place the ramekins on a baking sheet and bake for 20 minutes. Turn the baking sheet and bake for another 20 minutes. The strata is done when the tops are golden brown and they have risen very high. Turn out and place right side up onto individual plates. Garnish with a sprig of sage.

Makes 6 servings.

HUEVOS VERDE

This is a lighter version of the traditional Huevos Rancheros. It's creamy polenta with salsa verde, a lightly poached egg, and black beans.

Begin the black beans the day before serving; make the polenta at least 4 hours or the day before serving.

Preheat the oven to 200°F. Place the polenta triangles on a baking sheet and warm for 10 minutes in the oven. In a small saucepan heat the beans on low.

Remove the bulk of the cilantro stems. Place the tomatillo sauce and remaining cilantro in a small food processor. Blend until the cilantro is chopped.

In a wide but fairly shallow pot, bring about 4 inches of water and the vinegar to a boil.

Poach the eggs (see page 176) and put them in a dish just big enough to hold all the eggs. Cover with foil.

On each plate place 2 polenta triangles and about ⅓ cup beans next to the triangles. Prop 1 poached egg on the beans and cover with the salsa verde. Sprinkle with the queso fresco. Serve immediately.

Makes 6 servings.

12 Polenta Triangles (recipe follows)

2 cups Black Beans, cooked (recipe follows)

½ bunch cilantro, washed

2 cups tomatillo sauce (see page 179)

3 tablespoons vinegar

6 eggs

¼ cup finely grated queso fresco

Polenta Triangles

2 cups water

½ teaspoon salt

½ cup yellow cornmeal

1 tablespoon butter

⅓ cup whole milk

¼ cup Romano

Bring the water and salt to a boil in a medium saucepan. To avoid clumping add the cornmeal in a steady stream while continuously whisking. When the mixture starts to bubble, reduce the heat to a simmer and cook for 7 to 10 minutes, stirring frequently. Turn off the heat and allow the polenta to rest for about 10 minutes. Add the butter, milk, and Romano and cook on low for another 5 minutes, stirring constantly.

Line a 9-by-14-inch casserole with parchment. Pour in the polenta and let stand for 20 minutes; refrigerate for at least 4 hours or overnight. Turn out the polenta, remove the parchment, and cut into 3-inch triangles. Extra polenta can be wrapped in plastic and frozen for up to 3 months.

Makes about 3 cups, or about 18 triangles.

Black Beans

2 cups dried black beans

1 sweet onion, diced

2 teaspoons ground cumin

1 teaspoon kosher salt

Cover the beans with at least 3 inches of water and soak overnight. Rinse the beans and strain. In a heavy medium pot or slow cooker, place the onion, beans, salt, and enough water to cover 2 inches above the beans. Bring to a boil; decrease heat and simmer for 3 hours.

Makes about 6 cups.

ANGEL HAIR NOODLE KUGEL

We like to highlight Willamette Valley Cheese Eola Jack in this dish, but any good Jack is fine. Fresh herbs are a must for their delicate flavor. We like to make the kugel in individual servings for presentation, but if you are doing a casual family breakfast, you can make it in an 8-by-10 inch casserole.

Preheat the oven to 350°F and oil six 6-ounce ramekins with baking spray. Cook the pasta in salted boiling water for about 3 to 4 minutes, strain, and rinse with cold water. Set aside.

Slice the tomatoes lengthwise into thirds and remove the seeds and centers. Set aside.

In a large bowl whisk the eggs until light and airy. Add the flour, salt, and baking powder and beat again. Stir in the cottage cheese, Jack cheese, and butter. Add the basil, parsley, thyme, and half the scallions, and mix.

Put ⅓ cup pasta in each ramekin. Top with ½ cup egg mixture and mix with a fork, distributing the egg evenly through the pasta. Top with 1 tomato slice skin side up and a few scallion around the tomato. Place the ramekins on a baking sheet and bake for 30 to 35 minutes or until set in the middle. Holding each ramekin with an oven mitt and a towel to catch the kugel, turn out each one and place right side up on individual plates. Serve immediately.

Makes 4 to 6 servings.

2½ ounces uncooked angel hair pasta (2 cups cooked)

2 Roma tomatoes

5 eggs

¼ cup all-purpose flour

¼ teaspoon salt, plus additional for pasta

½ teaspoon baking powder

8 ounces cottage cheese

6 ounces shredded Jack cheese

½ stick (¼ cup) melted unsalted butter

1 teaspoon finely chopped fresh basil

1 teaspoon finely chopped fresh Italian parsley

¼ teaspoon finely chopped fresh thyme

2 scallions, thinly sliced through the light green part, divided

Willamette Valley Gouda, Leek, and Potato Strudel

At the Strudel House we had a daily savory strudel and often for brunch we made strudel with eggs. After it is baked and cooled it is very good cut into squares for a luncheon appetizer. We have found savory strudel is good with a puff pastry rather than with the dough used for sweet strudel. The puff pastry should be made with all butter. Find it in the freezer sections of specialty stores or online.

1 medium russet potato

2 medium leeks

2 tablespoons clarified butter (see page 175)

Kosher salt

Freshly ground pepper

1 11-by-11-inch puff pastry sheet (keep in freezer)

8 eggs plus 1 egg separated, reserving the white

3 cups half & half

1 tablespoon butter

2 ounces cream cheese

2 ounces (1 cup) shredded Gouda

¼ teaspoon water

Peel and cut the potato into ⅓-inch dice. Soak in water and set aside.

Rinse the leeks and shake them dry. Starting at the root end, slice them ½ inch thick until they start to get woody, just past the pale green part. Discard the woody parts. Rinse the leeks again if dirt is present and set aside in a colander to dry. Drain the water from the potatoes and spin them in a salad spinner until fairly dry or lay them out on a clean towel and pat dry. Cook the leeks and potato in the clarified butter over medium-low heat until the potato is cooked through and both are slightly browned. Season with the salt and pepper. Set aside.

Remove the puff pastry from the freezer and let it thaw on a lightly floured surface for about 10 minutes or until soft and pliable. Roll the pastry until it reaches 11 by 15 inches. Place the 15-inch side horizontally on the work surface.

Preheat the oven to 450°F and oil a baking sheet with baking spray. In a large mixing bowl beat the eggs and egg yolk with a whisk. Mix in the half & half and a pinch of salt; whip again.

In a nonstick skillet over medium-low heat, heat the 1 tablespoon of butter. When hot add the eggs. Cook the eggs very slowly using a rubber spatula to stir while they cook. (Do not let the eggs get too hot too quickly or they will lose their custardlike consistency.) Before the eggs start to hold their shape, remove the skillet from the heat and add the cream cheese in small bits around the edges. Return the skillet to the heat and fold the cream cheese into the eggs. Cook the eggs only until they start to hold a shape. They shouldn't run at all, but do not overcook or they will be dry. When their consistency is like a very soft custard, remove from the heat. Fold in the Gouda but do not mix thoroughly. Let the eggs sit for about 5 to 10 minutes to cool.

Whisk the reserved egg white and the water to make an egg wash and baste a 1½-inch border around the bottom and sides and a 4-inch border on the top of the pastry. The next steps must be done quickly so the pastry does not get too warm. Spread the eggs over the pastry. Spread the potato and leeks evenly over the eggs. Fold the left and right borders in toward the middle; starting at the bottom gently roll up the strudel, being careful not to let the egg move up too much. Grab the top of the pastry and pull and stretch it over to make a roll. Make sure the sides stay in while you roll. Roll the strudel over so the seam is on the bottom. Cradle the strudel in your forearm and gently move it onto the baking sheet. Baste the top with the remaining egg wash.

Bake for 25 minutes. Let rest for 20 minutes. Slice with a serrated knife and serve.

Makes 8 to 10 servings.

SWEET CORN FRITTERS

4 egg yolks

¼ cup whole milk

1 cup fresh sweet corn,
cooked and cut off the cob

1 teaspoon salt

Dash cayenne

3 tablespoons all-purpose flour

2 teaspoons clarified butter
(see page 175)

We serve these tasty fritters with any egg dish or just by themselves. Always make enough for seconds.

Whisk the egg yolks and add the milk. Stir to combine. Add the corn, salt, cayenne, and flour, and mix.

Heat the butter in a medium skillet. Drop the batter by tablespoons to make 2-inch fritters. Cook until both sides are golden brown.

Makes 20 fritters.

MEAT

WE ALWAYS SERVE the meat separate from the eggs for two reasons. First, our meats are of superior quality and taste, and they deserve a stage of their own. Second, we aim to please both vegetarians and carnivores. Most of our meats are made at Taylor's Sausage in Cave Junction, Oregon, and shipped directly to Heceta Head. Taylor's also custom makes some of our own recipes. We feel very fortunate to have such a wonderful sausage maker produce our meats for us. You'll find that many grocers now carry fresh sausages with interesting combinations of meats and flavors.

Making sausage and other charcuterie can be a very involved process or it can be as simple as making meat loaf—just put a little of this and a little of that in with the meat and cook until it's cooked through. Both practices are rewarding, but time and practice are certainly considerations. Carol grew up on a farm in Nebraska, and sausage making—using the entire animal in the process—was a regular activity for her Czech family. The grinder and sausage stuffer we use is at least 100 years old and still in good working condition.

Whether you have all day to make sausage or just a few minutes to toss some ingredients into ground meat and fry it up, we want our recipes to be approachable. For this reason we start the chapter with recipes that do not require a grinder. Most markets now provide ground meat or will grind it on request. Since the sausages in these recipes can be made the morning they are served and with little effort, we kept the amount needed to about one pound. Then we have a few recipes that do require a grinder. If you are going through the trouble of getting out the grinder, you might as well make five pounds and freeze some for later.

When we grind our meat, we prefer to season the meat with the spices and grind them together so the flavor is dispersed evenly throughout the meat. We like to start with whole spices and grind them ourselves. A mortar and pestle works well, but so does a blender. Most blenders now come with a small-jar attachment that works well for small amounts of herbs, nuts, and so on. A small-mouthed canning jar will usually screw onto a blender too.

At your local market it may be easier to find the meat already ground, so we will explain how to use already-ground meat to make these recipes. It is much easier to form these sausages into patties rather than stuffing them into casings. Patties should be about ⅓ inch thick and cooked in clarified butter on medium heat until they are browned on both sides.

If you stuff fresh sausage into larger casings or buy fresh sausages at your market, they will need to be simmered before browning or grilled very slowly until they are cooked through. To simmer, fill a skillet with about 2 inches of water and bring to a boil. Add the sausages and reduce the heat to a simmer over medium-low heat. Simmer for about 3 minutes; turn them over and simmer for another 3 minutes. Turn off the heat, drain the water completely, and return the pan to the burner to evaporate the remaining moisture. When the sausages are dry, add clarified butter to coat them. Turn the heat to medium or medium low. Cook until they are nicely browned on both sides. Cut and serve immediately.

If you are preparing fresh sausage in small casings, such as Taylor's Chicken Apple and Cherry (see page 185 to contact Taylor's), you do not need to simmer them. If they are 1 inch or smaller in diameter, cook them directly on medium low until they are nicely browned on both sides. Before serving cut one open to be sure it has cooked through.

VOGELTANZ SAUSAGE

This sausage is named after Carol's son, Dan. He created this rub for pork tenderloin and we have adapted it for our breakfast sausage. Dan also serves the pork with a side of avocado, apple, and cilantro, and a glass of red wine, of course.

For information about making sausage, read "The Meat Course" introduction, pages 118–19.

Grind the salt, cumin, oregano, pepper, and cayenne together and add to the meat with the wine. Refrigerate for at least 2 hours.

To serve, form the meat mixture into patties and brown on both sides. Serve with the avocado mixture.

Makes about 6 to 9 servings.

1½ teaspoons salt

½ teaspoon whole cumin

½ teaspoon dried oregano

¼ teaspoon freshly ground black pepper

Pinch cayenne

1 pound ground pork

¼ cup dry red wine, preferably Cabernet Sauvignon

Avocado Mash (recipe follows)

Avocado Mash

Cut the avocado into ½-inch dice. Peel, core, and cut the apple into ⅓-inch dice. Mix the avocado and apple with the cilantro. Add salt to taste. Refrigerate until ready to serve.

Makes about 2 cups.

2 avocados

1 Fuji apple

2 tablespoons chopped fresh cilantro

½ teaspoon salt

SuDan Farms Greek Lamb Sausage

Sue and Dan Wilson raise lamb in Canby, Oregon. Every dish we make with their lamb just melts in your mouth. This sausage is outstanding with the Spinach, Japanese Kale, and Juniper Grove Feta Frittata.

For information about making sausage, read "The Meat Course" introduction, pages 118–19.

1 pound ground lamb

2 tablespoons pine nuts

1 tablespoon finely chopped kalamata olives

1 teaspoon minced fresh mint

½ teaspoon freshly ground black pepper

1 teaspoon salt

¼ teaspoon ground cinnamon

¼ teaspoon ground allspice

¼ teaspoon lemon zest (see page 184)

2 tablespoons lemon juice

Mix the lamb, nuts, olives, mint, pepper, salt, cinnamon, allspice, zest, and lemon juice. Refrigerate 2 hours or overnight.

To serve, form the mixture into patties and brown on both sides in a skillet over medium heat until cooked through.

Makes about 1 pound.

ROASTED GARLIC CHICKEN SAUSAGE

The mild taste of roasted garlic makes this sausage nice for mornings, and it is delicate enough to serve with eggs and Oregon truffles. It is also nice with pasta and fresh garden vegetables.

For information about making sausage, read "The Meat Course" introduction, pages 118–19.

Mix the garlic, chicken, mustard, parsley, capers, wine, salt, pepper, and bread crumbs. Refrigerate 2 hours or overnight.

To serve, form into patties and brown on both sides in a skillet over medium heat until cooked through.

Makes about 1 pound.

8 cloves garlic, roasted and mashed
(see page 178)

1 pound ground chicken

2 teaspoons Dijon mustard

2 teaspoons chopped
fresh Italian parsley

1 tablespoon capers

2 tablespoons dry white wine
or vermouth

¾ teaspoon salt

½ teaspoon white pepper

¼ cup fresh bread crumbs
(see page 175)

1 pound ground turkey

1 cup fresh pumpkin, roasted
(see page 178)

1½ tablespoons grated shallot

2 teaspoons fresh marjoram

2 pinches ground cloves

1 teaspoon salt

½ teaspoon paprika

¼ teaspoon freshly ground black pepper

2 tablespoons sweet white wine

3 tablespoons fresh bread crumbs
(see page 175)

Cranberry Relish (recipe follows)

3 cups fresh cranberries

1 jalapeño, seeded and coarsely chopped

½ bunch cilantro, stemmed

1 cup sugar

Zest from ½ lime (see page 184)

Juice from 1 lime

THANKSGIVING SAUSAGE

For years our family always tried something new for the obligatory cranberry relish —until Carol made this fresh relish with a bit of jalapeño, cilantro, and lime. Now we make the relish several times a year to accompany a variety of dishes and sandwiches as well as our turkey and pumpkin sausage.

For information about making sausage, read "The Meat Course" introduction, pages 118–19. Prepare the cranberry relish several hours before serving.

Mix the turkey, pumpkin, shallot, marjoram, cloves, salt, paprika, pepper, wine, and bread crumbs. Refrigerate 2 hours or overnight.

Form into patties and brown on both sides in a skillet over medium heat. Serve with the relish.

Makes about 1 pound.

Cranberry Relish

In a small food processor combine the cranberries, jalapeño, and cilantro; pulse to a relish consistency. Mix in the sugar, zest, and lime juice; refrigerate for several hours before serving.

Makes about 4¼ cups.

THAI COCONUT GREEN CURRY CHICKEN SAUSAGE

When Michelle and Steven traveled in Thailand, they came upon a campground on the island of Phuket. Though Phuket is the most visited island, the Phuket campground was a secluded paradise. A young couple raised shrimp on the oceanfront property and they built a kitchen to host meals for travelers who wanted to camp on the beach. While Steven drank whiskey with the owner of the campground and listened to him play American classics on his guitar, Michelle was back in the kitchen with his wife, Tim (she shortened her long Thai name!). Michelle soaked up as much knowledge as she could about Thai cooking. One of her best finds: powdered coconut. This product is just what it claims to be—coconut ground to a powder and packaged ready to use. It is brilliant because you can make the curry as thick as you like and make only as much as you need for the moment. The curry in the recipe is also the best curry brand available, besides making your own.

For information about making sausage, read "The Meat Course" introduction, pages 118–19.

1 pound ground chicken

3 teaspoons Maesri Green Curry
(see page 182)

¼ cup coconut powder (see page 181)

2 teaspoons scallions, thinly sliced
to the dark green part

1½ teaspoons chopped fresh cilantro

1½ teaspoons soy sauce

¼ teaspoon sugar

Mix the chicken, curry, coconut powder, scallions, cilantro, soy sauce, and sugar. Refrigerate 2 hours or overnight.

To serve, form into patties and brown on both sides in a skillet over medium heat.

Makes about 1 pound.

BUFFALO SWEDISH STYLE POTATO SAUSAGE

This sausage is an all-time favorite for slicing and grilling because the potato turns crispy, like hash browns. You will need your own grinder for this sausage because we recommend grinding the milk-soaked bread with the meat a couple of times to make it really smooth. Buffalo is readily available in Oregon and we prefer it to beef. It is really lean and very rich but not gamey. If buffalo is not available, beef can be substituted.

For information about making sausage, read "The Meat Course" introduction, pages 118–19.

Grate the potatoes with a large-hole grater and cook them in boiling water until they are almost soft. Drain and set aside.

In a large bowl, soak the bread in the milk. Set aside.

Cut the buffalo and pork into 3-inch cubes; combine them and add the allspice, ginger, pepper, and salt. Mix and refrigerate until well chilled.

Squeeze the milk out of the bread; discard the milk. Grind the bread, meat and spice mixture, and onions together twice. Fold in the potato. Stuff into casings or form into patties. Use the sausage within 3 days or freeze for up to 3 months.

To cook the sausage in casing, they will need to be simmered before browning. To simmer, fill a skillet with about 2 inches of water and bring to a boil. Add the sausages and reduce the heat to a simmer over medium-low heat. Simmer for about 2 minutes; turn them over and simmer for another minute. Turn off the heat, drain the water completely, and return the pan to the burner to evaporate the remaining moisture. When the sausages are dry, remove them from the pan and cut them at an angle into four pieces. The inside will look underdone. Add clarified butter to the skillet and when melted return the sausage to the skillet cut side down. Cook on medium heat until they are nicely browned on both sides and cooked through. Serve immediately.

Makes about 2½ pounds.

1 pound 4 ounces (about 2½ cups) potatoes

1 loaf French or other light white bread

4 cups whole milk

6 ounces buffalo roast

10 ounces pork roast

1¼ teaspoons ground allspice

1¼ teaspoons ground ginger

1¼ teaspoons freshly ground black pepper

5 teaspoons kosher salt

2 sweet onions, quartered

CREPINETTE

When Michelle lived in Walla Walla, Washington, she was given an opportunity to do charcuterie with a man flown from France to butcher four pigs and teach Michelle's friend how to make sausages. What a grand time! Roget was so talented. He had been a butcher for 40-plus years, and this trip was his first time out of France. It was quite the adventure for him as well. All the recipes were exceptional, but Crepinette was Michelle's favorite.

Crepinette is named for the lacey pork intestinal lining, or caul fat, used as a casing. Caul fat really makes the sausage because it keeps the flavors sealed in and tenderly cooks the meat. Caul fat can be found at your local butcher shop.

For information about making sausage, read "The Meat Course" introduction, pages 118–19.

2½ pounds caul fat

5 pounds pork meat and fat (about ⅔ meat to ⅓ fat)

3 tablespoons chopped fresh parsley

3 small shallots

½ sweet onion

5 teaspoons kosher salt

2 teaspoons freshly ground pepper

1 tablespoon clarified butter (see page 175)

Soak the caul fat in cold water for about 1 hour. Cut into 6-inch pieces and set aside.

Cut the pork and fat into 2- to 3-inch pieces. Add the parsley, shallots, onion, salt, and pepper; mix well and refrigerate 2 to 3 hours.

Grind the meat very fine. Roll into billiard ball–size balls. Place in the middle of the caul fat and gather the sides together, pushing down to make a patty about 4 inches in diameter. Repeat with all the meat.

Refrigerate and use within 3 days or freeze for up to 2 months. To cook the patties, place them in a skillet over medium-low heat with a little of the butter. Heat slowly until they are cooked through and nicely browned on both sides, about 6 or 7 minutes on each side.

Makes 24 patties.

JATERNICE

This is an old Czech recipe from Carol's childhood. Her parents made jater-nice every winter with hog heads, hearts, tongues, and snouts. If the whole pig was not available, her family used pork roast without the fat removed.

For information about making sausage, read "The Meat Course" introduction, pages 118–19.

Cut the meat into fist-size chunks. In a large pot cover the pork with water and 2 teaspoons of the salt. Bring to a boil and simmer until tender, about 1½ to 2 hours. Remove the pork from the broth and set aside to cool. Reserve the broth in a shallow pan to cool.

Chop the onion into 1-inch dice. Sauté in the butter until browned. Set aside.

Cut the bread into large chunks and soak in the pork broth for about 5 minutes. Set the grinder for a fine grind. Squeeze any extra moisture out of the bread and grind the bread.

In a large bowl, mix the pork, onion, bread, garlic, the remaining 5 teaspoons of salt, allspice, marjoram, poultry seasoning, and pepper. Mix thoroughly and grind. Put the sausage into casings or portion into 3-ounces patties. Refrigerate and use within 3 days or freeze for up to 2 months.

To cook the sausage in casings, they will need to be simmered before browning or grilled very slowly until they are cooked through. To sim-mer, fill a skillet with about 2 inches of water and bring to a boil. Add the sausages and reduce the heat to a simmer over medium-low heat. Simmer for about 3 minutes; turn them over and simmer for another 3 minutes. Turn off the heat, drain the water completely, and return the pan to the burner to evaporate the remaining moisture. When the sausages are dry, add clarified butter to coat them and with a knife cut a small slice in each sausage to prevent them from popping open. Turn the heat to medium low. Cook until they are nicely browned on both sides. Cut and serve immediately.

Makes about 5½ pounds.

5 pounds pork roast

7 teaspoons kosher salt, divided

1 large onion

1 tablespoon butter

1 loaf French or other light white bread

6 cloves garlic

1 teaspoon ground allspice

5 teaspoons dried marjoram

1 teaspoon poultry seasoning

2 teaspoons freshly ground black pepper

CRISPY OVEN ALDER-SMOKED PEPPER BACON

There are many types of bacon; our favorite is a thick peppered bacon. For groups of two or twenty, we find that baking bacon in the oven cooks the fastest, most even, and cleanest way possible. At our table we usually bake about two pieces per person, but good bacon is hard to pass up. If you are not preparing all seven courses, you may want to make three pieces each.

Preheat the oven to 350°F. Lay the bacon slices side by side on a rimmed baking sheet, overlapping a bit if necessary but not laying pieces on top of each other. Bake for 10 minutes. Using tongs, turn the bacon over. Make sure it is browning evenly. Rearrange slices if they are getting too done in some places and not enough in others. Do not drain off any fat or the bacon will dry out. Bake for another 10 minutes. After 5 minutes check for hot spots again and rearrange if necessary. Bacon is done when it looks slightly overcooked, which will ensure crispiness. Taking it out too early will create limp bacon.

When the bacon is cooked, stack it on a platter with paper towels between the layers. Keep it in a warm oven until ready to serve. To serve, put the bacon on a warm serving platter and serve with decorative tongs.

James Beard's Liver Pâté

James Beard lived in Lake Oswego, Oregon, not far from the Strudel House and visited the restaurant a few times. Mike had a chat with him one day about the elaborate process Carol would go through to make traditional chicken liver pâté. After lunch Beard handed Mike a note that had this recipe on it and told him it is just as good and takes a fifth of the time to make. We served this pâté for 15 years at the restaurant. It was a favorite on our brunch menu.

6 ounces liverwurst

6 ounces cream cheese

1 teaspoon dry sherry

½ teaspoon Worcestershire sauce

½ teaspoon dried tarragon

Pinch fines herbes

2 cloves garlic, minced

1 tablespoon whole green peppercorns

In a mixer combine the liverwurst, cream cheese, sherry, Worcestershire sauce, tarragon, fines herbes, and garlic; blend well, stopping to scrape down the sides and bottom. When smooth, fold in the peppercorns.

Serve with sliced baguette, butter, Dijon mustard, shaved red onion, and cornichons.

Makes about 1 pound.

DESSERT

WE'VE SAVED THE BEST for last—well, almost last. Just two more courses to go! Many of these desserts are old family recipes, and many were regulars at the Strudel House.

If there is one favorite pastime Carol has, it's desserts—not so much eating them but making them for eager and very happy recipients. Although Carol is retired, even now she can't stop making desserts for our guests.

At the B&B we use a convection oven for most of our baking. Convection ovens circulate the air, which produces even baking and light, flaky pastries. Convections also increase the oven temperature by 15 to 20 degrees. In this book we have adjusted the recipes for non-convection ovens, so if you are using a convection oven, reduce the recipe temperature accordingly. See more baking tips and cooking techniques on page 175.

RUGELACH

These Yiddish pastries are wonderful to serve at a tea or luncheon. They can be made quite small or large, depending on how big you cut them. For breakfast we make them slightly larger than usual and warm them just before serving. Our favorite rugelach filling is the Oregon hazelnut and currant. You can also use your favorite preserves as a filling or any nut and spice combination that sounds good to you.

Each filling recipe makes enough for two disks, so you can choose two fillings per recipe of dough.

8 ounces cream cheese,
at room temperature

1 cup unsalted butter, chilled

½ teaspoon salt

2 cups all-purpose flour

Filling (recipes follow)

2 egg yolks

2 teaspoons water

In a mixer with a paddle attachment, combine the cream cheese and butter until fairly smooth. Add the salt and slowly add the flour until well mixed. Separate into 4 pieces, shape into disks, and cover with plastic wrap. Refrigerate at least 2 hours or overnight.

Preheat the oven to 350°F. Cover a baking sheet with aluminum foil, oil with baking spray, and set aside. Prepare the filling.

On a lightly floured surface, roll 1 disk into a 12-inch circle. Add the filling. Using a pizza cutter or sharp knife, cut the circle into 12 to 16 wedges, depending on the size you wish to make the rugelach.

To make the rugelach shape, take 1 section and pull it from the disk so it is not part of the circle. Beginning at the wide part, roll the section toward the point. Place it on the baking sheet point side down. Roll the remaining sections.

Whisk the egg yolks and water together. With a pastry brush, baste the top of each rugelach. Bake for 15 minutes and turn the backing sheet. Bake for another 15 minutes or until the rugelach is golden brown. Remove and let cool on a wire rack.

Makes 48 medium size or 64 small rugelach.

Poppy Seed Rugelach

Mix the poppy seed, cream, sugar, and vanilla. Divide the mixture and spread half on each of 2 disks.

Fills 2 disks.

⅓ cup poppy seed, ground (see page 177)

2 tablespoons heavy cream (see page 181)

3 tablespoons sugar

¼ teaspoon vanilla extract

Hazelnut Currant Rugelach

Combine the sugar and cinnamon. Set aside.

Brush each disk with 1 tablespoon of the butter. Sprinkle each disk with half the sugar and cinnamon mixture. Spread on the currants and nuts gently with your hand to even them out. With a rolling pin gently press the filling into the dough so it will stick.

Fills 2 disks.

⅓ cup sugar

2 teaspoons ground cinnamon

2 tablespoons unsalted butter, melted, divided

½ cup currants

¾ cup hazelnuts, finely chopped

Almond Rugelach

Mix the almond paste, corn syrup, and water. Spread half the mixture on each of 2 disks.

Fills 2 disks.

½ cup almond paste

2 tablespoons corn syrup

1 tablespoon warm water

Pear Tart

Mike hates to serve this tart to our guests. The only way he will agree to serve it is if we agree to make a tart just for him. This is light and simple. It is one of the best ways we know how to show off our Oregon state fruit.

½ cup unsalted butter

2 cups all-purpose flour

1 teaspoon salt

4 to 5 tablespoons ice water

Filling (recipe follows)

Topping (recipe follows)

Lightly sweetened whipped heavy cream, for garnish (see page 180)

Freshly ground nutmeg, for garnish

In a large bowl, cut the butter into the flour and salt until it is a crumble. Using your fingers gently stir in 4 tablespoons of the ice water. If the dough comes together without crumbling, you will not need the last tablespoon of water. If it still crumbles, add the remaining 1 tablespoon of water. Bring the dough together without working it too much or it will become tough. Form into a disk, cover with plastic wrap, and refrigerate until chilled, at least 1 hour.

Preheat the oven to 400°F. On a lightly floured surface, roll out the pastry to about 13 inches in diameter for a 12-inch tart pan. Fold the dough in half and slide it over the tart pan. Unfold the dough and gently press the edges into the pan. Do not over-compress the dough or it will shrink and become tough when it bakes. Arrange the pears evenly on the unbaked shell and cover with the topping. Bake for 45 minutes.

Serve at room temperature with the whipped cream and the nutmeg.

Makes 8 to 10 servings.

8 cups Bartlett or Comice pears

½ cup sugar

2 teaspoons lemon zest, grated (see page 184)

4 tablespoons lemon juice

¼ cup small tapioca

Filling
Peel, core, and slice the pears ⅛ inch thick. Toss with the sugar, zest, lemon juice, and tapioca.

¾ cup all-purpose flour

¾ cup sugar

1 teaspoon grated fresh ginger

¾ teaspoon ground cinnamon

¼ teaspoon mace

¼ cup butter

Topping
In a medium bowl, mix the flour, sugar, ginger, cinnamon, and mace. Cut in the butter until a crumble forms.

LEMON ALMOND POLENTA CAKE

This year we purchased about 200 lemons from Morning Glory Farm in Walton, Oregon. Yes, lemons in Oregon! They are so sweet you could eat them like you eat an orange. What we can't use fresh we candy, zest, and juice, and freeze so throughout the winter we can savor every drop. This dessert is a delicate approach to using such fine lemons.

Good polenta is steel cut and fresh. Some polenta is too coarse for this recipe, and food processors tend to just toss it around. Many blenders, however, come with small, jarlike attachments that grind it fine enough. Most small-mouth canning jars also fit blenders.

෴

½ cup sliced almonds

¾ cup plus 2 tablespoons unsalted butter, divided

¾ cup plus 1 tablespoon sugar, divided

½ cup polenta, finely ground

½ cup all-purpose flour

2 tablespoons cornstarch

1 teaspoon baking powder

1 teaspoon salt

½ cup almond paste

3 large eggs

Zest from 1 lemon, finely grated (see page 184)

3 tablespoons lemon juice

½ teaspoon vanilla extract

Preheat the oven to 325°F. Place parchment on the bottom of a 9-inch cake pan. Sprinkle the almonds into the pan and bake for 10 to 12 minutes until toasted.

Melt 2 tablespoons of the butter and drizzle it with 1 tablespoon of the sugar over the almonds to coat. Spread the almonds evenly across the pan and set aside.

Combine the polenta, flour, cornstarch, baking powder, and salt. Set aside.

In a mixing bowl, mix the remaining ¾ cup of butter and ¾ cup of sugar until light. Add the almond paste and mix. Add the eggs one at a time; scrape down the sides and bottom after adding the last egg. Add the zest, lemon juice, and vanilla. Add the polenta mixture and mix only until combined.

Pour the batter over the almonds and smooth the surface with a spatula. Bake for 45 minutes. Cool in the pan on a wire rack for 20 minutes. Turn the cake onto a plate and peel off the parchment.

If you are serving the cake at a buffet or would like to show it off before cutting, a stencil and powdered sugar creates a showy centerpiece. Cut out a design from construction paper and place it on the cake. Dust with powdered sugar and carefully lift off the stencil, being careful not to tilt it until you are away from the cake.

Makes 8 to 10 servings.

MARIE'S CZECH STRUDEL

It seems every culture in Europe has a claim on strudel. This one comes straight from the Czech Republic, where Carol's grandparents were born and raised. Having had the Strudel House for 20 years, Carol made a lot of strudel, so much so that she ended up with carpal tunnel syndrome in both wrists. The key to really good strudel is getting the pastry as thin as possible. This entails rolling, gently pulling, and stretching the dough.

Begin making the dough at least several hours before serving.

Mix the flour and salt in a mixing bowl. Cut in the butter until a crumble forms. Set aside.

Beat the egg yolk, add the water, and add to the flour mixture. Using the paddle attachment, mix on low until the dough is smooth, shiny, and pulls away from the bowl. Form the dough into a disk. Wrap in plastic wrap and refrigerate until well chilled, several hours or overnight.

Prepare the filling before rolling out the dough and set aside. (After you roll out the dough, it must be filled immediately so the dough doesn't dry out and become brittle.)

On an even, lightly floured surface or pastry cloth, start rolling the dough straight up and down until it is 10 inches long. Pick up the dough and gently pull until it is about 14 inches long. Place the dough on the work surface again, this time with the long part horizontal. Roll again, pushing out and down to create a rectangle that will eventually measure about 18 by 15 inches. Add a little flour if necessary to keep the dough from sticking to the work surface. When the dough measures about 15 by 12 inches, it will become too difficult to roll. Gently pull the dough with your palm to get it as thin as possible.

Makes about 10 servings.

1 cup all-purpose flour

¼ teaspoon kosher salt

¼ cup unsalted butter

1 egg yolk

¼ cup warm water

APPLE STRUDEL

Oregon apples at their finest! Serve the strudel hot with good vanilla bean ice cream, and you are in for a special old-world treat.

Marie's Czech Strudel (see page 141)

6 medium Braeburn apples or other good cooking apples

¼ cup unsalted butter, melted

2 tablespoons cream, divided

1½ cups fresh bread crumbs (see page 175)

1 cup plus 2 tablespoons sugar, divided

1 tablespoon ground cinnamon

Lightly sweetened whipped cream or ice cream

Preheat the oven to 400°F. Line a baking sheet with parchment paper and oil with baking spray. Set aside.

Peel, core, and slice the apples into ¼-inch wedges. Measure the butter, cream, bread crumbs, 1 cup of the sugar, and cinnamon and have them ready to use.

Roll out the dough. Dust off any extra flour from the dough. Drizzle the butter over the pastry. With a pastry bush gently coat the pastry, reserving a 1-inch border. Baste the border with the cream and set aside the remaining cream for basting the top.

On the buttered area, evenly cover the pastry with the bread crumbs, apples, sugar, and cinnamon. Fold the left and right edges of the dough over the apples about 1½ inches. This will keep the juices from running out after it's rolled and while baking. Starting at the bottom gently roll the pastry toward the top. As you roll, gently brush off any excess flour from the pastry. Stop rolling when the seam is on the bottom.

Place the baking sheet next to the strudel and gently lift the strudel onto the sheet. Baste with the remaining cream and sprinkle with the remaining 2 tablespoons of sugar. Bake for 15 minutes. Reduce the temperature to 350°F and bake for 45 minutes.

Serve warm or at room temperature, alone or with the whipped cream or ice cream.

Makes about 10 servings.

MARIONBERRY CHEESE STRUDEL

This strudel is made with an Oregon original, the marionberry—a combination of Chehalem and olallieberry blackberries. Marionberries are big, juicy, and jammy and have an earthy undertone. If you can't find them, use any berry, apricots, or just cheese. This recipe is a Carol Korgan original and was the most popular dessert at the restaurant.

Note: Add the last 12 ounces of cream cheese at the end, just before filling the dough. If it is mixed in earlier, the filling becomes too soft and difficult to handle.

Preheat the oven to 400°F. Mix 1 pound of the cream cheese until smooth. Combine 1 cup of the sugar and flour; add to the cream cheese. Add the egg yolks, lemon extract, vanilla, and sour cream. Stop to scrape down the sides and bottom with a spatula. Mix again until smooth.

Oil the ring of a 9-inch springform pan with baking spray. Do not use the bottom of the pan. Cover a baking sheet with parchment paper. Clamp the springform, set it on the parchment, and trace a circle around its edge to use as a guide. Turn over the parchment. You should still be able to see the tracing. Oil the circle with baking spray and set aside. Open the springform and set aside.

Add the remaining 12 ounces of cream cheese to the mixer and mix until smooth.

Roll out the dough. Leaving a 1-inch border on the sides and bottom and a 4-inch border on the top, spread the cream cheese mixture evenly using a rubber spatula. Sprinkle on the berries. Baste the borders with some of the cream.

Starting at the bottom roll the pastry toward the top. Stop with the seam side down. Gently move the strudel to the parchment so it fits in the drawn circle. Tuck one end into the other, like putting your hand in your opposite sleeve.

Place the springform over the strudel and clamp it closed. Baste the strudel with the remaining cream and sprinkle with the remaining 2 tablespoons of sugar. Bake for 20 minutes. Reduce the heat to 350°F and bake for 35 to 40 minutes until nicely browned and bubbly in the middle. Let cool completely in the pan.

To remove from the pan, run a metal spatula or knife along the sides to prevent sticking. Refrigerate or serve at room temperature.

Makes about 12 servings.

Marie's Czech Strudel (see page 141)

1 pound plus 12 ounces cream cheese, divided

1 cup plus 2 tablespoons sugar, divided

⅓ cup all-purpose flour

2 egg yolks

½ teaspoon lemon extract

1 teaspoon vanilla extract

2 tablespoons sour cream

1¼ cups marionberries

2 tablespoons cream, divided

POPPY SEED STRUDEL

Playing devil's advocate one day while they were baking, Michelle asked Carol, "Why do we like poppy seed so much? They don't have a lot of flavor." Carol's reply: "What are you talking about? They are full of flavor. You haven't experienced the true taste of poppy seed until you take one poppy right out of the garden, cut the top off, and shake all the poppy seeds into your mouth. Mmmm." This Czech classic is in honor of Carol's favorite seed. It also happens to be her favorite flower and the name of Michelle's dog.

We have a grinder from the Czech Republic just for grinding poppy seed. To grind your own, see page 177.

Preheat the oven to 350°F and oil a Bundt pan with baking spray. Sprinkle 1 tablespoon of the poppy seed and 1 teaspoon of the sugar into the pan and set aside.

In a small saucepan, heat the milk. Add the raisins and set aside to cool for 10 minutes.

Grind the remaining 1½ cups of poppy seed; put them in a mixing bowl with the applesauce, the remaining 1 cup of sugar, almond extract, vanilla, salt, milk and raisins. Mix well with the paddle attachment, stopping to scrape down the sides and bottom. Add the bread crumbs and mix briefly. Set aside.

Roll out the dough. Brush with the butter; spread the poppy seed mixture over the butter, leaving a ½-inch border on the sides and a 3-inch border at the top. Roll up the strudel away from you. Pick up the strudel by the ends and place it in the Bundt pan with the seam side up. Tuck one end into the other end, like putting your hand in your opposite sleeve.

Bake for 1 hour. Remove from the oven and let cool on a wire rack for 30 minutes. Turn onto a cake plate and let cool. Serve 2 or 3 very thin slices, about ½ inch thick per serving.

Makes about 12 servings.

Marie's Czech Strudel (see page 141)

1½ cups plus 1 tablespoon poppy seed, divided

1 cup plus 1 teaspoon sugar, divided

¾ cup whole milk

1 cup raisins

1¾ cups applesauce, preferably chunky

1 teaspoon almond extract

1 teaspoon vanilla extract

¼ teaspoon salt

1 cup bread crumbs (see page 175)

¼ cup butter, melted

MARIE'S KOLACHES

Marie was the kolache queen. For all family functions she would make kolaches, sometimes in the hundreds. At home she kept quite a variety in the freezer, so she could pull them out and serve them warmed when an unexpected guest stopped by. With more than 80 grandkids and great-grandkids, that was a regular occurrence. We are not sure if she planned it, but we were amazed to find she had made such an ample supply that every person at her funeral was able to enjoy one last kolache from Grandmother Marie.

✍

1 cup whole milk

¼ cup sugar

¼ cup plus 1 tablespoon unsalted butter, divided

1 teaspoon salt

¼ cup cooked and mashed potato

2 large egg yolks

1 package (2 ¼ teaspoons) yeast

¼ cup lukewarm water

1 teaspoon sugar

Pinch ground ginger

3 ½ cups all-purpose flour, divided

3 tablespoons unsalted butter, melted

Fillings (recipes follow)

Icing (recipe follows)

Turn the oven to its lowest heat setting. In a small saucepan, heat the milk almost to a boil. Remove from the heat and add the sugar, ¼ cup of the butter, and salt; stir until the butter is melted. When it is lukewarm, add the potato and egg yolks. Set aside.

Turn off the oven.

In a mixing bowl, dissolve the yeast in the water. Mix in one teaspoon of the sugar and ginger and let sit until bubbly. Add ¼ cup of the flour and mix. Add the milk mixture and mix until combined. Add the remaining 3 ¼ cups of flour and mix for 3 minutes. Pat the dough with the remaining 1 tablespoon of butter and cover with a cloth. Place in the warm oven (but turned off) to let rise until doubled, about 1 hour.

Oil a baking sheet with baking spray and set aside.

Knead the dough for about 3 minutes to release the air. Dust your hands with flour and pull off golf ball–size portions of the dough. With your hands cupped, roll the portions between your palms; using your thumbs as a guide, form nicely rounded balls. Place them on the baking sheet about 1 ½ inches apart. Brush with the melted butter, and with both index fingers make a quarter-size indentation in the middle of each ball. Cover the baking sheet with a cloth and place it back in the still-warm oven or other warm, draft-free space. Let rise for 15 minutes or until doubled in size. Make the same quarter-size indentation again and fill with the desired filling. Let rise in a warm place for 15 minutes.

Preheat the oven to 425°F. Bake for 10 to 12 minutes, until golden brown. Remove from the oven and place the pan on a wire rack. Baste the sides of the kolache with the melted butter while they are still hot.

When cool dust the kolache with powdered sugar or dab each with
the icing.

Makes about 3 dozen.

Cherry Filling

Drain the cherries, reserving the juice. Pour 1 cup of the juice in a small
saucepan; add the sugar. Bring to a boil over medium-high heat.

Place 2 tablespoons of the juice in a small bowl and mix with the cornstarch. Remove the saucepan from the burner and immediately add the
cornstarch mixture. Return the saucepan to medium heat and stir to
thicken. Add the cherries, almond extract, salt, and butter. Return to the
heat and let simmer. The mixture should be thick enough so it will stay
on the kolache. Let the sauce cool. Fill each kolache indentation with
the mixture, including about 3 whole cherries.

Fills 3 dozen.

3 cups canned whole cherries and juice

2 tablespoons sugar

5 teaspoons cornstarch

⅛ teaspoon almond extract

Pinch salt

1 teaspoon unsalted butter

Prune and Cottage Cheese Filling

In a small saucepan over high heat, bring the prunes, 2 tablespoons of
the sugar, 1 pinch of the salt, and 1 cup of the water to a boil; reduce the
heat to medium low and simmer for 15 minutes. Add the cinnamon and
lemon juice and mix with a fork until smooth and the consistency is like
fruit preserves. If it is too stiff, add a little water; if it is too thin, simmer
until reduced to the correct consistency. Set aside.

Squeeze the cottage cheese through cheesecloth to drain off as much liquid as possible. Mix the cottage cheese with the egg yolk, the remaining
2 tablespoons of sugar, vanilla, and the remaining 1 pinch of salt.

Put 1½ teaspoons of the cottage cheese mixture in the center of each
kolache, stretching the indentation so the filling does not run over the
sides. Top with about ½ teaspoon of the prune mixture.

Fills about 3 dozen.

*1 cup (about 6 ounces) prunes,
pitted and chopped*

4 tablespoons sugar, divided

2 pinches salt, divided

1 cup water, plus additional

¼ teaspoon ground cinnamon

1 tablespoon lemon juice

1 cup small curd cottage cheese

1 egg yolk

Dash vanilla extract

Icing

In a mixing bowl cream the butter, sugar, and almond extract until light.
Add 1 tablespoon of milk and mix. Add more milk to make the icing
spreadable but do not make it runny.

Ices about 3 dozen.

1½ cups powdered sugar

¼ cup unsalted butter, soft

1 drop almond extract

1 to 2 tablespoons whole milk

CRANBERRY UPSIDE-DOWN CAKE

This dessert deserves a real sweet tooth. Like baklava and mead, the honey is rich and seductive. Because it is a such a star performer, be sure you use good-quality light honey, like clover or orange blossom. We also use Cape Blanco Cranberries. They are vine ripened, which produces the sweetest tart berry ever.

¼ cup plus 2 tablespoons unsalted butter, divided

1½ cups cranberries, fresh or frozen

6 tablespoons light honey (see page 182)

2 teaspoons water

½ teaspoon ground cinnamon

1 cup all-purpose flour

1 teaspoon baking powder

½ teaspoon baking soda

¼ teaspoon salt

4 ounces cream cheese

½ cup sugar

1 large egg

½ teaspoon vanilla extract

¼ cup whole milk

Lightly sweetened whipped heavy cream (see page 180)

Line a 9-inch cake pan with parchment and oil with baking spray. Set aside.

In a large skillet heat ¼ cup of the butter; when the butter is hot, add the cranberries. Toss to coat, about 1 minute. Add the honey, water, and cinnamon; cook over medium- low heat until the berries start to burst, about 2 or 3 minutes. With a slotted spoon, remove the berries and place them in the cake pan. Return the skillet to medium heat and reduce the remaining liquid until syrupy, about 2 minutes. Pour the syrup over the cranberries. Set aside.

Preheat the oven to 350°F. In a medium bowl mix the flour, baking powder, baking soda, and salt. Set aside.

In a mixing bowl, cream together the cream cheese, the remaining 2 tablespoons of butter, sugar, and egg, stopping to scrape down the sides and bottom. Add the vanilla, milk, and flour mixture last. Mix just to combine. Spoon the mixture over the cranberries, but do not mix. Smooth to the edges with a spatula. Bake for 30 to 35 minutes.

The cake is done when a toothpick inserted in the center comes out clean. Let cool in the pan 15 minutes on a wire rack. Loosen around the edges of the pan with a metal spatula and invert onto a 10-inch or larger cake plate. Garnish with the whipped cream. Serve warm or at room temperature.

Makes 8 to 10 servings.

CREAMY LEMON TART

As Mike would say, this dessert makes you go "Whaaa!" All our recipes are only as good as their ingredients, and this one is no exception. The farm fresh eggs and locally grown lemon makes this tart almost too bright to look at. Go ahead; eat with your eyes closed!

Preheat the oven to 350°F. Have a 9-inch fluted tart pan with removable bottom available.

In a large mixing bowl combine the flour, almonds, sugar, and salt. With a pastry cutter, cut in the butter until the mixture is crumbly. Add the water; form the dough into a ball using your fingers to work it together.

Starting with the sides, press the pastry into the pan, then cover the bottom. Bake for 15 minutes. Set aside to cool; reduce the oven temperature to 325°F.

Pour the filling into the tart crust. Bake for 25 to 30 minutes, until it appears to be set, not runny or jiggling in the middle, but do not let it brown on top.

Cool completely; refrigerate for several hours to chill completely. Serve with the whipped cream and lemon slices.

Makes 8 to 10 servings.

Filling
With a wire whisk, mix the egg yolks, sugar, butter, condensed milk, zest, lemon juice, and salt. (Using the whisk will reduce the chance of bubbles forming.)

¾ cup all-purpose flour

¼ cup almonds, ground

¼ cup powdered sugar

¼ teaspoon salt

¼ cup unsalted butter

1 tablespoon ice water

Filling (recipe follows)

Lightly sweetened whipped heavy cream (see page 180)

Fresh lemon slices

4 egg yolks

3 tablespoons sugar

6 tablespoons unsalted butter, melted

¾ cup sweetened condensed milk

2 teaspoons finely grated lemon zest (see page 184)

¾ cup freshly squeezed lemon juice

Pinch salt

OREGON BERRY CRISP
WITH WASSON BROTHERS RASPBERRY WINE

This is a very comforting all-year recipe, and the wine adds a layer of sophistication. At the B&B we use the recipe as a template, yet we can't help but throw in a handful of cake crumbs from a leftover coffee cake or candied hazelnuts left from a salad served the previous evening. If you add ingredients as we do, add ¼ cup of butter and 2 tablespoons of brown sugar for each ½ cup of added dry ingredients.

The Wasson Brothers Winery makes very velvety sweet wines that are almost a syrup. They are wonderful on ice cream and crepes too. (See page 176.)

Wash the strawberries, blueberries, and marionberries in a colander and let sit until almost dry.

Combine the oats, ⅓ cup of the flour, brown sugar, salt, cinnamon, and ginger in a food processor. Pulse to blend and break down the oats a bit. Add the butter and pulse until a crumble forms. Set aside. Preheat the oven to 350°F.

Hull and slice the strawberries; mix with the other berries. Sprinkle the remaining 4 teaspoons of flour and the ⅓ cup of sugar over the berries and gently mix. Divide the berries among six 4-ounce ramekins. Top each with 1 tablespoon of the wine and about 2 tablespoons of the crisp.

Place the ramekins on a baking sheet and bake for 25 minutes. Check for doneness; crisps are done when the berries are bubbling and the tops look brown and crispy.

Makes 6 servings.

1 cup strawberries

½ cup blueberries

½ cup marionberries

½ cup rolled oats

⅓ cup plus 4 teaspoons all-purpose flour, divided

½ cup brown sugar

½ teaspoon salt

1 teaspoon ground cinnamon

½ teaspoon ground ginger

¼ cup unsalted butter, chilled

⅓ cup sugar

6 tablespoons raspberry wine, divided

WILD HUCKLEBERRY CRUMB CAKE

The coastal huckleberry grows widely but is tedious to cultivate. It takes a patient person to gather enough of these flavorful berries to make a cake. We have a local jam maker who sells them to us canned in quart jars. He said, "Don't mention my name in your book. My pickers barely fill my needs for the season." Sorry we can't give you a source! If huckleberries are not available, try other berries or even peaches or pears.

2 cups fresh or canned huckleberries

2 cups all-purpose flour

2½ teaspoons baking powder

½ teaspoon salt

¾ cup butter

1 teaspoon vanilla extract

¾ cup sugar

1 large egg

¾ teaspoon finely grated orange zest (see page 184)

½ cup whole milk

Topping (recipe follows)

If you are using canned huckleberries, strain them and let them drain.

Preheat the oven to 350°F. Cut parchment to fit the bottom of a 9-by-9-inch pan; oil the sides and bottom with baking spray. Set aside.

Sift flour, baking powder, and salt. Set aside.

In a mixer cream the butter, add the vanilla and sugar, and beat until fluffy. Scrape down the sides and bottom and mix again. Add the egg and zest and mix until well blended. Add half the flour mixture, the milk, and the rest of the flour mixture. Fold in the huckleberries.

Pour the batter into the pan and cover with the topping. Bake for about 50 minutes. The cake is done when a toothpick inserted in the center comes out clean. Cool on a wire rack for 30 minutes. Run a knife around the sides of the pan to loosen any cake from the edges. Turn onto a baking sheet; turn over onto another baking sheet or serving plate.

Makes 10 to 12 servings.

½ cup brown sugar

½ cup all-purpose flour

¼ cup unsalted butter

Topping

Mix the brown sugar and flour. Cut in butter with a pastry cutter until a crumble forms.

Cheese Blintzes

These were an all-time favorite at the Strudel House and still are at the B&B.

Squeeze the cottage cheese through a double layer of cheesecloth and let it hang to drain. When the curds are fairly dry, place in a mixing bowl and mix with the cream cheese, powdered sugar, sour cream, zest, and vanilla. Set aside.

Spoon 2½ tablespoons of the filling in the center of each crepe. Fold like an envelope (bottom up, sides in) and roll up.

Melt the butter in a 12-inch skillet. Reduce the heat to medium low, add the blintzes, and cover with foil. Cook each side until lightly brown. Serve with a dollop of marionberry preserves, crème fraîche, and a shake of powdered sugar.

Makes 12 crepes.

1 cup small curd cottage cheese

4 ounces cream cheese

2 tablespoons powdered sugar

4 teaspoons sour cream

⅛ teaspoon finely grated orange zest (see page 184)

¼ teaspoon vanilla extract

1 recipe crepes (see page 176)

2 teaspoons clarified butter (see page 175)

Marionberry preserves

Crème fraîche (see page 176)

Sifted powdered sugar

MASCARPONE MARMALADE CREPES

These pretty crepes are easy to make and light enough to serve on a warm summer morning. The orange flower water is nice with the fresh tart taste of kiwi fruit.

Blend the mascarpone, crème fraîche, cream, and marmalade. Set aside.

Place a crepe on each dish and fill with about 1½ tablespoons of the mascarpone mixture. Fold the sides over and place another crepe beside it. Repeat the filling and folding. Garnish with small pieces of kiwi fruit, strawberry, and navel or blood orange. Top with the sauce. Serve immediately.

Makes 12 crepes.

⅓ cup mascarpone (see page 182)

2 tablespoons crème fraîche
(see page 176)

⅓ cup heavy cream (see page 181)

⅓ cup marmalade

1 recipe crepes (see page 176)

Kiwi fruit, strawberry, orange pieces,
for garnish

Sauce (recipe follows)

Sauce

Mix the marmalade and flower water; add enough water to make the sauce drizzle easily.

Makes about ¾ cup.

½ cup marmalade

2 tablespoons orange flower water
(see page 183)

1 to 2 tablespoons hot water

ELVIS PRESLEY POUND CAKE

A guest gave this recipe to Michelle many years ago; since then we have often seen it in print. The story goes that Elvis sometimes ate two of these cakes daily. We've tried to verify the story, but all we find are more bizarre eating habits of the King.

Oil three 8-by-4-inch pans with baking spray and set aside.

3 cups sugar

1 cup unsalted butter

7 large eggs

3 cups all-purpose flour

½ teaspoon salt

1 teaspoon baking powder

1 cup heavy cream (see page 181)

2 teaspoons vanilla extract

In a mixer with the paddle attachment, thoroughly cream the sugar and butter. Stop to scrape down the sides and bottom and mix again. Add the eggs one at a time, beating well after each addition.

Sift the flour, salt, and baking powder three times. Add half the flour mixture, the cream, and the remaining flour mixture. Add the vanilla. Mix on medium high for 5 minutes. Spoon the batter into the pans and put the pans on a baking sheet. Set the oven rack to the middle position.

Put the baking sheet in a **cold** oven. Heat the oven to 350°F. Bake for 60 minutes and check for doneness. The cakes are done when a toothpick inserted in the center of 2 cakes comes out clean. Cool in the pans on a wire rack for 30 minutes. Remove the cakes from the pans and place them on a wire rack to cool.

Cakes can be stored for several days in an airtight container. They also freeze well for up to three months.

Makes 3 cakes.

STRAWBERRY WALNUT CHEESE KUCHEN

Make this with your best preserves. We really like our house-made straw-berry jam, but all good preserves will shine in this dessert.

Oil a 10-inch springform pan and set aside. With a pastry cutter, blend the flour, sugar, and butter until a crumble forms. Measure 1 cup of the mixture, combine with the walnuts, and set aside.

Add the baking powder, baking soda, salt, sour cream, egg, and vanilla to the remaining flour mixture and mix just until blended. Spoon into the pan. With buttered fingers so the mixture doesn't stick to your hands, spread the mixture over the bottom and halfway up the sides of the pan.

Preheat the oven to 350°F. Prepare and pour the filling into the pan. Dapple the preserves around the edges of the kuchen, trying not to get too close to the middle or the middle may become soggy. Sprinkle the reserved crumble over the kuchen and bake for 55 minutes. Let cool in the pan for 1 hour. Run a metal spatula between the pan and the sides of the kuchen. Release the springform and place the kuchen on a cake plate. Serve at room temperature.

Makes 10 to 12 servings.

2 ¼ cups all-purpose flour

¾ cup sugar

¾ cup unsalted butter, plus additional

½ cup walnuts, chopped

½ teaspoon baking powder

½ teaspoon baking soda

½ teaspoon salt

¾ cup sour cream

1 large egg

1 teaspoon vanilla

Filling (recipe follows)

⅓ cup strawberry preserves

Filling

In a mixer with a whip attachment, mix the cream cheese and sugar until light. Add the egg, vanilla, and lemon extract. Mix until the filling is smooth and light.

8 ounces cream cheese, at room temperature

¼ cup sugar

1 large egg

½ teaspoon vanilla extract

¼ teaspoon lemon extract

ALMOND BUTTER CAKE

This cake is for the almond lover. It is very rich but not too sweet, and it has a texture that is dense but still moist. This cake is very good served with a well-aged Gouda and apricot preserves.

8 ounces almond paste

1 cup unsalted butter, softened

¼ cup sugar

2 large eggs

1 teaspoon vanilla extract

2 cups all-purpose flour

1 teaspoon baking powder

½ teaspoon salt

1 cup sour cream

¼ cup sliced almonds

Topping (recipe follows)

Preheat the oven to 325°F and generously oil one 12-inch Bundt pan or 10-inch tube pan with baking spray. Set aside.

In a large mixing bowl, mix the almond paste with the butter until it forms a crumble, stopping to scrape down the sides and bottom. Add the sugar and mix until light. Add the eggs one at a time. Add the vanilla. Scrape down the sides and bottom again and mix.

Measure the flour, baking powder, and salt into another bowl and mix with a spoon. Add to the almond paste mixture, alternating with the sour cream and ending with the flour mixture. Stir just to combine. Set aside.

Sprinkle the almonds evenly in the pan. Sprinkle the topping over the almonds. Pour the batter over the topping, being careful not to mix them, and bake for 55 to 60 minutes. The cake is done when a toothpick inserted in the center comes out clean. Let rest on a wire rack for 30 minutes. Turn out the cake and let it cool completely before slicing.

Makes 12 servings.

¼ cup brown sugar

¼ cup all-purpose flour

2 tablespoons unsalted butter

Topping

Mix the brown sugar and flour in a bowl or small food processor. Cut in the butter until the mixture is crumbly.

Cinnamon Nutmeg Coffee Cake

This is one of our favorites because it is light, not too sweet, and so moist. We like to serve it with Pink Lady apples, dulce de leche, and Tillamook® 3 Year Vintage White Extra Sharp Cheddar.

2 cups all-purpose flour

1 teaspoon baking soda

1 ½ teaspoons baking powder

¼ teaspoon salt

½ cup butter

1 cup sugar

2 large eggs

½ teaspoon vanilla extract

1 cup crème fraîche (see page 176)

Filling and Topping (recipe follows)

Preheat the oven to 350°F and place the oven rack in the center. Oil a 9 ½-inch deep-dish pie plate with baking spray. Set aside.

Sift the flour, baking soda, baking powder, and salt together and set aside.

Cream the butter until very light. Add the sugar, eggs, and vanilla. Mix well and stop to scrape down the sides and bottom. Mix again. Add the flour mixture, alternating with the crème fraîche and ending with the flour mixture. Do not overmix. The batter will be quite thick.

Spoon and spread half the cake batter into the pie plate. Add half the filling, then the remaining cake batter in the center. Do not smooth out or it will run over the sides while baking. Top with the remaining filling.

Bake for 25 minutes; turn the pie plate. Bake for 20 minutes more and check for doneness. The cake is done if a toothpick inserted in the center comes out clean. Let cool on a wire rack for about 20 minutes; turn out onto a serving plate. If you plan to serve it the next morning, wrap it in foil and refrigerate. In the morning place it in a 200°F oven, still wrapped in foil, for about 30 minutes before serving. Serve warm.

Makes 10 to 12 servings.

½ cup walnuts, finely chopped

½ cup brown sugar

1 ½ teaspoons ground cinnamon

5 shaves fresh ground nutmeg

Filling and Topping
Mix all ingredients together and set aside.

SOUR CHERRY DUMPLINGS

We use sour cherries right from our tree at home. They are very tart and smaller than sweet Bings. Depending on the size and sweetness of the cherries you use, you will want to adjust the amount of cherries and sugar in each dumpling. Although cherry is our favorite, we also fill them with fresh apricots or plums. We steam them in a bamboo steamer so we can do many layers at a time. If you don't have a bamboo steamer, steam them in batches.

Put 3 cups of the cherries in a heavy medium saucepan and cover with 1 cup of the sugar. Stir; place over medium-low heat. Bring to a slight boil; reduce to a simmer and simmer until the cherries have lost most of their liquid and a sauce has formed, about 25 minutes. Set aside to cool.

Place a wide (wide enough to hold the bamboo steamer) pot of water over high heat to boil. In a large bowl sift together the flour, baking powder, and salt. Work in the butter with the tips of your fingers to form a meal. Add the milk gradually, using a knife to slice it into the dough.

Turn the dough onto a floured surface and form it into a 6-by-6-inch square. Cut it into 12 pieces. Pat one piece until it is flat and rounded. Place 3 of the remaining cherries in the center and cover with ½ teaspoon of the remaining sugar. Fold the dough around the cherries, gather it, and pinch it closed. Set it aside and make the rest of the dumplings.

Oil the bamboo steamer generously with baking spray. Place the dumplings in the steamer seam side down and about ½ inch apart. Depending on the size of the steamer, more than one layer may be needed. Cover and steam for 12 minutes. Do not lift the cover.

Grind the poppy seed and mix with ¼ cup of the sugar. Serve the dumplings and pass the cherry sauce, melted butter, poppy seed mixture, remaining sugar, and cream.

Makes 12 dumplings.

4 cups sour cherries, pitted and divided

1¾ cups sugar, divided

2 cups all-purpose flour

4 teaspoons baking powder

½ teaspoon salt

2 tablespoons unsalted butter

¾ cup whole milk

¼ cup poppy seed (see page 177)

Melted butter

1 cup heavy cream (see page 181)

FRESH FRUIT TART
WITH OREGON HAZELNUT CRUST

These tarts take a little time, but they are not too difficult to make. They are a perfect summertime showcase for fresh fruit. Pick a selection of the ripest, brightest fruits and cut them into bite-size pieces. The crowd will go wild when they see these little gifts. They are almost too pretty to eat—almost.

※

½ cup hazelnuts, roasted (see page 178)

1 cup all-purpose flour

¼ cup sugar

½ teaspoon salt

¼ cup unsalted butter, chilled

1 large egg

1 recipe pastry cream (see page 177)

1 recipe whipped heavy cream (see page 180)

2 cups fresh berries and fruits, washed, peeled if necessary, and cut into bite-size pieces

Mint, for garnish

Preheat the oven to 350°F and oil eight 4-inch tart pans with baking spray. Finely chop the hazelnuts in a food processor.

In a medium bowl, combine the flour, sugar, and salt. Add the hazelnuts. Cut in the butter, form a well in the center, and add the egg. Cover the egg with the mixture and press it in toward the egg to mix. Work the mixture until it clumps together and forms a dough.

Roll the dough into an 8-inch log and cut into 8 equal proportions. Press each piece evenly on the bottom and up the sides of each tart pan. Put the pans on a baking sheet and bake for 20 minutes. Let cool on a wire rack for 15 minutes; remove the tarts from the pans.

Fill a medium pastry bag with the pastry cream; using a medium plain tip, fill each tart halfway. Fill a pastry bag with the whipped heavy cream; using a medium star tip, fill the tart, ending with a decorative swirl. Decorate the tops with an assortment of fresh fruits that complement one another in color and taste. Garnish with the mint. Chill until ready to serve.

Makes 8 servings.

BLUEBERRY PARFAITS

Fresh blueberries, tart lemon curd, and light génoise. In a decorative glass, it's an edible present.

Whipped heavy cream (see page 180)

Lemon Curd (recipe follows)

Génoise (recipe follows)

2 to 3 cups blueberries, washed

Citrus slivers

Using a medium star tip, fill a pastry bag with the whipped cream and set aside. Using a medium tube tip, fill another pastry bag with the lemon curd and set aside.

Using individual parfait glasses as a guide, cut 8 génoise pieces so they will fit perfectly in the center of each glass.

In the bottom of each glass, place 1 or 2 small pieces of génoise left over from the cut pieces. Pipe a layer of whipped cream over the génoise. Place a layer of blueberries on the cream. Pipe a layer of lemon curd over the berries, making sure to fill in the cracks. Cover with the cut génoise piece. Pipe on a layer of whipped cream and top with a layer of blueberries. Garnish with 2 citrus slivers.

Makes 8 to 10 parfaits.

5 large egg yolks

1 cup sugar

½ cup unsalted butter

1 tablespoon lemon zest (see page 184)

½ cup lemon juice (about 3 lemons)

Pinch salt

Lemon Curd

Place 2 inches of water in the bottom of a double boiler. Combine the egg yolks, sugar, butter, zest, lemon juice, and salt in the top of the double boiler. Over medium heat bring the water almost to a boil; stir the mixture constantly until it coats a wooden spoon evenly. Remove from the heat and let cool for 10 minutes. Place in a covered container and refrigerate until well chilled.

Makes about 2½ cups.

Hot water

3 large eggs

½ cup sugar

½ teaspoon vanilla extract

½ teaspoon lemon zest (see page 184)

½ cup cake flour, sifted

3 tablespoons unsalted butter, melted

Génoise

Preheat the oven to 350°F and place the oven rack in the center. Line a 9-by-13-inch pan with parchment and oil with baking spray. Set aside.

Put the eggs and sugar in a mixer bowl. Set aside. In another bowl, larger than the mixer bowl with the eggs and sugar, add enough hot water to fill it one-third full. Place the bowl with eggs and sugar in the hot water bath and whisk the eggs and sugar until they are lukewarm. Return the bowl to the mixer; with the whisk attachment, beat the eggs and sugar on high for 7 minutes. The volume should triple and should have the appearance of soft whipped cream. Gently mix in the vanilla and zest. Fold in half the flour, then the butter. Fold in the remaining flour.

Pour the batter over the oiled parchment and gently shake to smooth it. Bake for 15 to 18 minutes. The cake is done when a toothpick inserted in the center comes out clean. Let cool in the pan for 15 minutes. Turn the cake onto a wire rack and let cool completely.

Makes 8 to 10 parfaits.

TODD'S APPLE PANCAKE

There is a restaurant in Portland that Carol and Mike ate at so often during Carol's pregnancy with Michelle that Michelle is convinced she is part pancake. We all try to re-create the wonderful pancakes that we've had over the years from this special place. Carol and Mike's son, Todd, has been working on perfecting an apple pancake for about five years, and we think he finally nailed it.

This isn't your normal pancake. It is a rich custardlike pile of sautéed apple with brown sugar and cinnamon oozing in every direction.

3 Granny Smith apples, peeled, cored, and thinly sliced

½ cup butter

1 cup packed brown sugar

2 tablespoons ground cinnamon

6 large eggs

1 cup all-purpose flour

½ cup whole milk

½ cup half & half

⅛ teaspoon freshly ground nutmeg

½ teaspoon salt

In a 10-inch iron skillet, cook the apples, butter, brown sugar, and cinnamon over medium-high heat until the apples are al dente, about 10 minutes. Set aside to cool.

Preheat the oven to 450°F. Whisk the eggs in a large bowl. Add the flour and combine. Add the milk, half & half, nutmeg, and salt and combine.

Spread the apples evenly in the skillet. Pour the batter over the apples but do not mix. Bake for 20 minutes. Invert on a large serving platter, being very careful of the hot syrup. Cut into wedges and serve immediately.

Makes 12 small servings.

LAVENDER POT DE CRÈME

While visiting the San Juan Islands, Michelle found a culinary lavender that is intoxicating. This dessert was inspired by the lavender. It's perfect for Mother's Day or for a bridal luncheon. We serve it by itself or with a dab of rose jam on top.

Preheat the oven to 325°F and set aside eight 6-ounce ramekins. In a medium bowl, whisk the egg yolks and stir in the sugar. Set aside.

Put the cream, milk, and lavender in a medium saucepan and heat over medium heat until scalded. Strain the mixture through a fine-mesh sieve or cheesecloth into a large measuring cup with a pour spout. Discard the lavender.

While stirring, slowly add about 2 tablespoons of the cream mixture to the egg yolk mixture. When incorporated and still stirring, add ¼ cup of the cream mixture into the yolk mixture. Repeat until all the cream mixture is incorporated into the yolk mixture. Add the salt and mix. Pour the mixture into the measuring cup.

Place the ramekins in a baking dish with at least 3-inch-tall sides. Fill the ramekins with the cream mixture. Carefully fill the baking dish with enough of the boiling water to go halfway up the sides of the ramekins. Cover the dish with foil and carefully place it in the oven. Bake for 35 minutes or until just set. Remove from the oven, remove foil, and let cool in the water. Remove from the water and chill before serving.

Makes 8 servings.

8 large egg yolks

½ cup sugar

2 cups heavy cream (see page 181)

2 cups whole milk

¾ teaspoon culinary lavender (see page 185)

Pinch salt

Boiling water

FRUIT & CHEESE

IF WE FOLLOW THE EUROPEAN tradition of multicourse meals, what would be finer than to end them with a bit of artisan or farmstead cheese and fresh fruit. Oregon is well-known for its fruit, and now cheese makers are crafting some of the finest cheeses worldwide. Every year it seems there is a new cheese to discover, and this treasure hunt is the most rewarding.

The pairings that follow are examples of what we serve at the B&B. We hope they will inspire you to try new cheeses—local, regional, and of the world. We focus on Oregon cheese because there is so much to choose from, but please enjoy cheese from many places, for they all have their own distinct and pleasing qualities.

When you entertain, cheese is a great way to spark conversation and curiosity. When we host events, our most popular choice for an appetizer is the Oregon cheese platter. We always notice a group huddled around the cheese, talking, pointing, and, of course, tasting the different combinations.

The best way to get to know different kinds of cheese is by experimentation. If there is a local shop that carries a variety of cheese, ask the cheese monger for a taste of a different cheese every time you visit. Ask about the cheese: where it is made, how it is made, and how it is best served. If you want to share cheese at a party, ask for a selection of four or five cheeses that complement one another and serve them with a variety of fruits, nuts, honey, and perhaps mustard, depending on the cheeses selected. Another way to experiment is by going online. Several online cheese shops and cheese clubs help educate people on the great world of cheese. These shops ship directly to you; they should also supply you with information to share about the cheeses you purchase.

When we start breakfast in the morning, we pull the cheese out of the refrigerator, keep it covered, and allow it to come to room temperature by the time it is served as the last course. Serving cheese at room temperature allows the flavors to open and the texture to be just right. How we cut the cheese depends on what cheese we are serving. Cheese with a bloomy rind (like Brie and Camembert) we leave whole and start the serving process so the guests know how to continue. We usually leave chèvre in a log or pyramid as the cheese maker intended, and we cut semisoft cheese very thin, placing the slices next to the fruit that will accompany them. We make harder cheeses, like cheddar, into match-stick pieces so they are easily handled. And the very hard, aged cheese like Boerenkass we shave very fine so the subtle flavor is enhanced when it melts in the mouth.

Presenting each cheese to its best advantage enhances that cheese and makes the experience easy for your guests to enjoy.

Some of our favorite combinations:

Dutchman's Flat
Juniper Grove Farm

This is a mold-ripened chèvre. It has a very delicate, wrinkly rind and a creamy inside that is laced with ash. Try pairing this cheese with an apricot compote and fresh Bing cherries.

Redmondo
Juniper Grove Farm

Aged a minimum of nine months, this is a Pecorino-style cheese, like a Romano or a Parmesan. It is very firm, nutty, and buttery. We like to finely shave it and serve it with orange marmalade and pistachios.

Lavender Farmer's Cheese
Juniper Grove Farm

Of all the flavored cheeses, this has to be our all-time favorite. The lavender is musky and sensuous and the cheese is a little sweet—a wonderful combination. We slice it really thin and serve it with melon, pluots, or plums.

Mary's Peak
River's Edge Chèvre

This bold chèvre is a bloomy rind cheese that ages very nicely. It starts out very sliceable and ages to a consistency of heavy cream. We suggest serving it with Asian pear or Fuyu persimmon.

St. Olga
River's Edge Chèvre

St. Olga's rind is washed weekly in local beer, giving it a distinct taste and a beautiful, colored rind. It is excellent with raspberries and blackberries right off the vine. In winter serving it with a combination of Fuji apples and mango chutney is also stellar.

Siletz River Stones
River's Edge Chèvre

This hand-ladled Crottin is full flavored and spiked with green peppercorns. The spicy surprise joins nicely with a pomegranate syrup and the clean, crispy texture of Asian pears.

Crater Lake Blue
Rogue Creamery

This award-winning cheese is intense and complex with a beautiful blue vein running through it. We serve a nice hunk with pears and hazelnuts.

Oregonzola
Rogue Creamery

Our other favorite from the Rogue Creamery is this Gorgonzola-type cheese, aged at least 120 days and tangy and creamy too. A wedge of this cheese can be complemented by wildflower honey, hazelnuts, and red grapes roasted in grapeseed oil (see page 178).

Tillamook® 3 Year Vintage White Extra Sharp Cheddar
This cheddar has been aged for three years and it shows with its tang and texture. A favorite at the breakfast table, we serve it with slices of Pink Lady apple and dulce de leche (see page 176).

Boerenkass
Willamette Valley Cheese Company

A raw-milk, aged, Gouda-like cheese, Boerenkass is our favorite hard cheese. If truffles are in season, we like to shave the cheese and shave a bit of fresh truffle over the top with a slice of pear.

Havarti
Willamette Valley Cheese Company

A nice introductory cheese, this Havarti is mild, creamy yet still sophisticated enough to stand on its own. Try serving it in thin slices with dried cranberries, Honeycrisp apples, and walnuts.

THE BASICS

These recipes are variations of some classics that are staples in our kitchen. Many have several methods for making them; however, we tried to include the simplest and most straightforward ones. Also, in many recipes you may be able to vary the outcome by using local ingredients. We encourage experimenting with local flavorings, seasonings, and herbs.

Kitchen Insights

At the B&B we use a convection oven for most of our baking. Convection ovens circulate the air in the oven and produce even baking and light, flaky pastries. Convections also increase the oven temperature by 15 to 20 degrees. In this book we have adjusted the recipes for non-convection ovens, so if you are using a convection oven, reduce the recipe temperature accordingly.

When an oven rack is used, it should be placed in the center of the oven unless otherwise noted.

All baking recipes should be started with the ingredients at room temperature, unless otherwise noted.

Butter should be unsalted.

Eggs should large. Important note about raw egg consumption: We suggest caution in consuming raw and lightly cooked eggs due to the slight risk of salmonella or other food-borne illness. To reduce this risk, we recommend you use only fresh, properly refrigerated, clean eggs with intact shells, and avoid contact between the yolks or whites and the shell.

Extracts such as vanilla and lemon are real, not imitation.

Use kosher salt for cooking and sea salt for baking. Kosher salt doesn't sift well and the granules are too big for crusts.

Bread Crumbs

1 loaf French or Italian Bread

Preheat oven to 250°F. Split the bread lengthwise down the middle and place it on a baking sheet. Put in oven for about 2 hours checking every 30 minutes to make sure the bread is not browning. When the bread is completely dry, remove from the oven and place chunks in a large food processor. Process on high until crumbs form. Store crumbs in the refrigerator for up to one week, or in the freezer in a tightly sealed container for up to 2 months.

Clarified Butter

1 pound unsalted butter

In a small saucepan over low heat, slowly melt the butter completely. The milk solids will naturally separate and settle in the bottom of the pan, leaving the clarified butter in the middle and a fine crust on the top. With a spoon skim off the top layer and discard. Very carefully pour off the clarified butter into a sealable container. When the milk solids are almost joining the clarified butter, stop and let the solids settle for a moment. With a turkey baster or food injector, slowly skim any clarified butter from the top without getting milk solids. Add to the container; discard the milk solids, or save and add them in place of some liquid in bread recipes.

Makes about 1 ¾ cups.

Crème Fraîche

Crème fraîche is cultured heavy cream. It is available in specialty stores but is also very simple to make. We prefer crème fraîche to sour cream for its richness and versatility.

Bring 2 tablespoons sour cream and 1 cup heavy cream to room temperature and mix. Let stand at room temperature for 24 hours, which allows the sour cream cultures to act on the cream. Refrigerate for at least 4 hours and serve when chilled and set.

Makes about 1 cup.

Crepes

2 large eggs

6 tablespoons all-purpose flour

½ cup whole milk

4 teaspoons butter, clarified, melted and divided (see page 175)

½ teaspoon sugar

Pinch salt

With a whisk mix the eggs, flour, milk, 2 teaspoons of the clarified butter, sugar, and salt in a large bowl.

Heat a 7-inch nonstick skillet over low heat. Put a few drops of butter in the pan and wipe lightly with a paper towel. Add 2 tablespoons of the batter and tilt the pan so the batter completely covers the bottom evenly. Cook on one side only just until set, about 2 minutes; do not brown. Cool and stack in sets of four between wax paper.

Makes 12 crepes.

Dulce de Leche

A friend came back from South America with this secret familiar to all the old ladies. When you taste it, you'd think someone had worked all day to make this rich and smooth caramel. Guess again.

1 can sweetened condensed milk, unopened.

In a large heavy pot bring enough water to a boil to cover the can at least 3 inches. Immerse the unopened can in the water and boil for 3 hours. Check every 20 to 30 minutes to make sure the water is completely covering the can. Use extreme caution: If the can is not completely submerged in the water it could explode. Turn off the heat and remove the cans when cool. Open the can and enjoy!

Egg Poaching

Bring the desired number of eggs to poach to room temperature. Fill a wide pot (with sides about 5 inches high) with water and bring to a boil. Add 1 tablespoon white vinegar for each quart of water. Have a narrow dish with high sides and a cover ready at the stove. (A small Pyrex baking dish and foil works well.) Crack one egg into a one-cup measure careful not to break the yolk. Reduce the water to a gentle boil. Slowly tilt the measuring cup over the water and release the egg into the water. Repeat with eggs until there is about 2 inches of space between each egg. Increase the heat if the water is not at a gentle boil or reduce the heat if it is a rapid boil. Poach the eggs for about 5 minutes. Using a slotted spoon remove the first egg and check for doneness. The whites should be cooked and the yolk should be very runny. Place the eggs in the dish and cover until ready to use. To serve use a spoon and drain any extra water off the egg before placing them on the plate.

Freezing Berries

In the summer we get a very concentrated season of berries from all over Oregon. Knowing how much we will miss their presence in the winter, we try to preserve as many as possible. Preserves and sauces are always useful and appreciated, but sometimes we just want the berries for baking and other desserts. So we freeze them. We have found the best way to do this is individually frozen berries. We buy the berries by the flat. Wash them with a fine spray in a sieve and let sit to dry. Then cover baking sheets lined with parchment with berries and lay the sheets flat in the freezer until frozen, but not longer or the berries may get freezer burn. Place the berries in good quality freezer bags with as much air taken from the bag as possible. The berries will be ready for use and easy to handle individually. Some berries hold up better once thawed. For example, the marionberry was created for its ability to be frozen and thawed yet maintain its beautiful structure.

Grinding Poppy Seed

There are several ways to grind poppy seed. Our favorite is with a poppy seed grinder. Some blenders come with a small-jar attachment, or you can also use a small canning jar screwed onto your blender. Don't use a conventional food processor because it doesn't really grind. Ground poppy seed is like a somewhat dry paste and has released its aroma.

Pastry Cream

6 extra-large egg yolks

¾ cup sugar

3 tablespoons cornstarch

2 cups whole milk

2 tablespoons unsalted butter

1 teaspoon vanilla extract

2 tablespoons heavy cream (see page 181)

1 teaspoon cognac or other liqueur

Beat the egg yolks and sugar in a mixer on high for 3 minutes or until the mixture is pale yellow. Add the cornstarch and mix.

In a heavy saucepan, bring the milk just to a boil; immediately remove from the heat. With the mixer on low, gradually add the milk to the egg mixture. Scrape down the sides and bottom of the bowl with a rubber spatula and mix on low for 1 minute.

Return the mixture to the saucepan, cook on medium-low heat, and stir frequently with a whisk until the mixture thickens and evenly coats a wooden spoon, about 10 to 12 minutes. Remove from the heat and mix in the butter, vanilla, cream, and cognac. Strain into a bowl using a fine-mesh strainer. Cover and refrigerate until cool.

Makes 2½ cups.

Roasting

GARLIC

Preheat the oven to 350°F. Using a paring knife and starting about a third of the way toward the stem of the bulb, shave off the sides and top, leaving as much garlic intact but exposing as many cloves as possible. Reserve the cut garlic for another use.

Coat the bulb in olive oil and place it in a baking dish with enough broth or water to cover about ⅓ inch from the bottom. Cover with foil and bake for about 35 minutes or until the cloves are soft. Remove the foil and bake 10 minutes. Remove from the oven and let cool. Reserve the liquid for another use.

To remove all the roasted garlic, when cool squeeze the bulb into a dish. Cover and refrigerate for up to 4 days.

GRAPES IN GRAPESEED OIL

After picking the grapes from the vine, wash them and set aside until they are completely dry. Preheat the oven to 350° F. Drizzle grapeseed oil over the grapes and toss to coat. Place on a baking sheet and roast for about 30 minutes.

HAZELNUTS

Turn the broiler to high. Place the hazelnuts on a baking sheet about 6 to 8 inches from the top. Watch them carefully so they brown evenly and do not become over-toasted. When they are done, the skins will start to come away.

Remove the hazelnuts from the oven and let cool for at least 10 minutes. Place them in a paper bag and rub them from the outside of the bag, being careful not to tear it. Try to remove as much skin as possible.

After the nuts are roasted, they will become rancid more quickly. Use them within 1 month or freeze them in an airtight container for up to 3 months.

PEPPERS

Turn the broiler to high. Wash and dry the peppers. Place them on a baking sheet about 4 to 5 inches from the top of the oven. Turn them when the skin is black and blistered. When they are completely blackened, place them in a pot with a tight-fitting cover for about 10 minutes. This will steam the peppers and make the skins easier to remove.

Remove the skins, tops, and seeds. Strain any pepper juice that has collected; store the peppers with their juice in a sealed container and refrigerate for up to 5 days or freeze for up to 3 months.

PUMPKIN

Pumpkins come in many varieties. Some of our favorites are Musque de Provence, sugar bear, and kabocha. Technically, pumpkin refers to the shape of the squash; some very delicious varieties are not your typical jack-o-lantern pumpkins and some are not even orange. Ask at your local farmers' market or a farmer to distinguish which are best for eating. Ask about their sweetness, color, and moisture content.

Preheat the oven to 400°F. With a cleaver or other large knife, cut the pumpkin in half. With the tip of a spoon scrape out the seeds and stringy insides until just the flesh is left. Place on a baking sheet cut side up and bake for 30 to 60 minutes, depending on the size of the pieces. They are roasted when the flesh is soft and scoops easily. Remove from the oven and allow to cool completely.

Remove the rind and any dry spots on the surface of the flesh. In a food processor or blender, puree the flesh. Refrigerate for up to 4 days or freeze in 2-cup freezer containers for up to 3 months.

2 fresh Anaheim peppers, stemmed, roasted, and skins removed

1½ pounds tomatillos, husks removed and washed

3 cloves garlic

1 tablespoon fresh lime juice

Tomatillo Sauce

Place the peppers, tomatillos, garlic, and lime juice in a food processor and blend until smooth.

Makes 3 cups.

Wasson Bothers Raspberry Wine Sauce

This sauce is great served with many desserts. Two of our favorites are with blintzes and the Elvis Presley Pound Cake. If you like a jammy sauce, leave in the seeds. If you like a smooth sauce, pass it through a mill after stirring in the wine.

3 teaspoons cornstarch

1 tablespoon cold water

1 cup marionberries or blackberries

1 cup blueberries

½ cup sugar

⅓ cup Wasson Brothers Raspberry Wine or other sweet berry dessert wine or brandy

Mix the cornstarch and water in a small bowl until smooth. Set aside.

Put the marionberries, blueberries, and sugar in a medium saucepan and stir. Over medium-low heat, let the mixture reduce while stirring occasionally. After about 20 minutes, increase the heat to high to bring the mixture to a boil. Remove it from the heat, stir the cornstarch and water again and add it to the berries and mix thoroughly. Return to a boil and stir until it becomes thicker. Turn off the heat and let the mixture sit for 5 minutes. (The sauce will be a little thicker than you will want.) Add the wine and stir until incorporated.

Refrigerate for 5 days or freeze for 2 months.

Makes about 2½ cups.

Whipped Heavy Cream

Depending on the dish you are making, the amount of sugar you use will vary. For some very sweet or chocolatey desserts, we use very little to no sugar; for a lemon tart we might be very liberal. This recipe is for average sweetness. Adjust it according to the dish you are preparing.

1 cup heavy cream, very cold
(see page 181)

1 tablespoon powdered sugar, sifted

Place the cream in a very cold mixing bowl. Mix on medium high until it starts to thicken. With the mixer on low, add the powdered sugar; turn the mixer to high until soft to medium peaks form. Chill and use within 6 hours.

Makes 2 cups.

SPECIAL INGREDIENTS GLOSSARY

Aioli

Though there are many variations to this thick and creamy sauce the main ingredients consist of garlic, oil, and sometimes egg and lemon. It is commonly served with cold vegetables and grilled meats.

Candied Ginger

Candied—sometimes referred to as crystallized—ginger is sweet and chewy that can vary in strength and cut, with or without sugar. For many of our recipes, we use small chunks that are softer and easier to blend. The round slivers will also do, but many need extra blending. Most health food stores and specialty markets carry candied ginger.

Coconut Powder

Just as the name describes, it is powdered coconut. Read the label before buying because some have added sugar or are just coconut-flavored powder. Coconut powder is fantastic for any application that calls for coconut milk when fresh coconut is not available. Just reconstitute to the desired consistency.

Elderflower Syrup

A native plant in the Northwest, blue elderberry is quite tannic; treated properly, it can be used for a variety of dishes. In season we pick the blossoms for tempura and the berries for a great vinaigrette. The flower essence gives us a unique flavoring for berries and crepes. Although we have been unable to find a local crafter of elderflower syrup, we have found it in Norwegian and Swedish shops.

Heavy Cream

Heavy cream has a 36 to 40 percent fat content; light whipping cream has 30 to 36 percent. We prefer heavy cream because of the rich, silky taste we can't get with light whipping cream in certain sauces and desserts. Chill the cream well before whipping and it will double in volume.

Herbs

We use fresh herbs when they are available; we grow herbs to dry and use in the winter months. If fresh herbs aren't available, remember that dry herbs are two-thirds stronger than fresh. If you don't have garden space, it is easy and gratifying to grow a small pot of herbs right in the kitchen. Many markets now have fresh herbs all year-round.

Honey

Honey production is very bountiful in Oregon and on the West Coast. Farmers' markets and specialty stores are eager to sell locally produced honey that comes in many varieties. Many Oregon farms specialize, using honey from bees that have collected pollen from select flowers such as blackberry, Willamette Valley wildflowers, and fireweed. This gives the honey a very distinct flavor that will change the quality of each recipe.

Lox

Nova style lox is salmon that has been lightly brined, cold smoked, and very thinly sliced. See Resources, page 185.

Madras Curry Powder

This is a rather spicy curry from Southern India. It consists of many spices blended together with ground curry leaves as the main ingredient. It is traditionally used to flavor a main dish of chicken and vegetables served with rice and chutney. We like this particular one for its spicy quality. It makes a great seasoning for spreads, chicken salad, and sauces. This and many other curries can be found in most Asian markets.

Maesri Curry

This brand of curry is the closest to fresh that we have found. The green variety has no hidden additives or preservatives, just ground green chilies, garlic, ginger shallots, lemon grass, limes leaves, and other spices. Maesri curry can be found in most Asian food stores.

Mango Chutney

This condiment is made from unripe mangos and is a cross between a relish and jam. It is sweet and traditionally served in Indian cuisine alongside spicy curry dishes. We enjoy this chutney in many different ways such as sauce flavorings or salad dressings. Mango chutney and many other types can be found in specialty food stores.

Mascarpone

Pronounced "mahs-car-PO-nay," this Italian cream is really a double or triple cream cheese. It is very spreadable and a nice addition to many desserts, crepes, or just with fresh fruit. Mascarpone can be found in many grocery or specialty stores.

Nutmeg

Although we prefer all our spices freshly ground, you may find many spices only in ground form. If you keep them fresh, they're acceptable. Nutmeg, though, is one spice we much prefer to grind ourselves, especially when it is the signature spice in the dish. Many kitchen stores now stock nutmeg grinders. Nutmeg can also be grated with a micro-plainer or the smallest setting of a box grater.

Orange Flower Water and Rose Water

These wonderfully fresh floral waters can be found in many Asian and Middle Eastern markets. Use them in a variety of dishes such as fruit salads, fresh fruit drinks, fruit mousses, and desserts, and even as a summer freshener for your skin on humid days. The waters can differ greatly from brand to brand, so be sure to check their potency before using in your recipe. If the water seems particularly strong adjust the recipe by adding half the amount called and then more if it doesn't seem overpowering. The price of the water will also fluctuate with its strength and brand.

Passion Fruit Syrup

The passion fruit has a very rich and exotic flavor with tones of mango, pineapple, and apricot. Fresh passion fruit may be difficult to find, but some Asian or specialty markets may carry syrup, frozen puree, or concentrate. We toss passion fruit with fresh fruits and add the syrup to drinks. The syrup is also wonderful drizzled over ice cream and summer cakes or added to a rum punch.

Shallots

A small, reddish brown variety of allium, shallots are slightly sweeter and more intense in flavor than most onions. Shallots are used in cuisines worldwide; they'll keep for months in a cool, dark, well-ventilated place.

Wakame

Wakame is a type of sea kelp that grows plentifully on ocean coasts worldwide. Like all edible seaweed, it is rich in essential fatty acids, vitamin C, and trace minerals. Wakame is a flavorful addition to many dishes including soups, salads, and pickles. When dried and reconstituted, it greatly expands in volume. It is easiest to cut with kitchen shears. When collecting wakame or other sea vegetables, be sure they are still growing and are in areas free of bacteria blooms or pollution.

White Chocolate Syrup

This syrup is one of many flavors in a line of syrups originally used to flavor Italian sodas, which consist of soda water, flavored syrup, and sometimes cream. They have become popular additions to many recipes. Many companies produce flavored syrups; our favorite is Monin with Torani as a second choice. Both companies have a vast variety of flavors to choose from and can be found in specialty shops or online. See Resources page 185.

Wild Mushrooms

Oregon is home to much edible fungus and at least one kind is ready to harvest each month of the year with summer to fall the most productive months. Among the most poplar mushrooms are the chanterelle, morel, oyster, and boletus. Take heed if you harvest your own that you are absolutely sure about identification. Many mushrooms are toxic and even deadly if consumed.

Wine

Oregon has such an abundance of exquisite berries and wines. When the two come together, we get some velvety dessert wines that we enjoy on their own and for dessert in sauces, over ice cream, or added to other drinks for a kick. Some of our favorites are marionberry, raspberry, and blackberry wines made by the Wasson Brothers. See Resources, page 185. Berry sauces and baked fruit crisps take on a complexity and richness that will make an old country favorite luxurious.

Zest

This is the very outer layer of the citrus rind. It is removed using a zesting tool, micro-plainer, pairing knife or the smallest setting of a box grater. Remove as much rind with the least amount of pith (white part) attached as possible. Zest adds an intense citrus essence to many different dishes.

Dagoba Organic Chocolate
1105 Benson Way
Ashland, OR 97520
www.dagobachocolate.com
800-393-6075

GloryBee Foods
Honey
120 N. Seneca
P.O. Box 2744
Eugene, OR 97402
www.glorybee.com
800-456-7923

Juniper Grove Cheese
2024 SW 58th St.
Redmond, OR 97756
www.junipergrovefarm.com
541-923-8353

Local Harvest
Locate local organic foods,
farmers' markets, food
information, etc.
www.localharvest.org

Local Ocean Seafood
Albacore tuna and
other seafood
P.O. Box 1957
213 SE Bay St.
Newport, OR 97365
www.localocean.net
541-574-7959

Mai's Asian Market
256 E Olive St., Ste. A
Newport, OR 97365
541-265-5868

Monin Gourmet Flavorings
www.moninstore.com
800-966-5225

Morning Glory Farm
19540 Hwy. 126
Walton, OR 97490
541-935-4093

Oregon Lox Co.
4828 West 11th Ave.
Eugene, OR 97402
www.oregonlox.com
800-233-1850

Pacific Farms USA, LP
Wasabi (Japanese horseradish)
P.O. Box 223
Florence, OR 97439
www.freshwasabi.com
800-927-2248

Pacific Shrimp Co.
209 SW Bay Blvd.
Newport, OR 97365
541-265-4215

Pelindaba
Culinary lavender
33 Hawthorne Ln.
Friday Harbor, WA 98250
www.pelindabalavender
866-819-1911

River's Edge Chèvre
6315 Logsden Rd.
Logsden, OR 97357
www.threeringfarm.com/
cheeseroom.htm
541-444-1362

*Schöndecken Coffee
Roasters*
6720 S.E. 16th Ave.
Portland, OR 97202
503-236-8234

*Springfield Creamery
Nancy's Yogurt*
29440 Airport Rd.
Eugene, OR 97402
www.nancysyogurt.com
541-689-2911

SuDan Farms
32285 S Kropf Rd.
Canby, OR 97013
503-651-5262

Taylor's Sausage
525 Watkins St.
P.O. Box 188
Cave Junction, OR 97523
www.taylorsausage.com
541-592-4189

Tillamook® Cheese
4175 Hwy. 101 North
Tillamook, OR 97141
www.tillamookcheese.com
503-815-1300

Umpqua Aquiculture Inc.
Oysters
723 Ork Rock Rd.
Winchester Bay, OR 97467
www.umpquaoysters.com
541-271-5684

Wasson Brothers Winery
41901 Hwy 26
Sandy, OR 97055
503-668-3124

Willamette Valley Cheese Co.
8105 Wallace Rd. NW
Salem, OR 97304
www.wvcheeseco.com
503-399-9806

Woodsman Native Nursery
Salal jelly and others
4385 Hwy 101
Florence, OR 97439
541-997-2252

INDEX